THE HOME

EXERCISE
AND DIET
PAT BAIKIE

OCTOPUS BOOKS

Contents

Self assessment 6

Shaping up 16

Exercise 24

Sleep & relaxation 58

Healthy eating 66

Slimming 80

Index 94

This edition published 1988 by
Octopus Books Limited
Michelin House
81 Fulham Road
London SW3 6RB

© Cathay Books 1984
ISBN 0-7064-3385-8

Printed in Hong Kong

EXERCISE
AND DIET

Introduction

This is the exercise and diet book for you if you appreciate that your figure is more than a set of measurements-in-the-round. It's the sum total of your height and weight – plus the way your pounds are distributed.

A good figure can be much more of an asset than a pretty face. It can be arresting and expressive, going as well as coming. From a distance, all the details of your appearance are fused in a silhouette, which is the first thing people register as you approach. The initial impression is sharpened by the way you walk and carry yourself. Apart from measurements in appealing proportions, what makes a figure attractive is suppleness, grace and pride of bearing. All these qualities belong to a body that is disciplined into shape and at the peak of health.

Diet and exercise are the key contributors. Literally everyone – fat, thin or just right – needs exercise. And whether you are fat or thin or just right can be regulated by what you eat. Granted that food is a biological necessity, when you regularly eat more than your body requires for health and energy, you are bound to become overweight. To change that, your daily food intake must be reduced to supply fewer calories than you need; in that way you will use up the reserve energy you carry around in each surplus pound.

The Home Library Book of Exercise and Diet provides you with all you need to know about looking great and keeping trim and healthy.

Pat Baikie

Self assessment

Body Image

The immediate impression of the kind of person you are is made by the way you look. Instant 'You' is visual, more potent than a thousand words and, rightly or wrongly, people will rate you accordingly. If your appearance is trim and pleasing, you begin with an advantage in dozens of situations – college interviews, job interviews, standing for office in club or class. There's some justice in this superficial appraisal, too: the care you take of yourself is an authentic indication of your self-esteem, an appreciation of your own worth. Don't confuse it with vanity, for they are very different.

What do you really know about yourself? If you have ever listened in wide-eyed wonder to a recording of your own voice, you know how difficult it can be to recognize the way you sound to the outside world. The same difficulty exists in recognizing the way you look to other people. You never see yourself from the back or in motion unless you have been taught to observe yourself as a singer, actress, dancer or fashion model does. Women tend to concentrate on their faces in a mirror as though their heads were disembodied. A sudden accidental glimpse of the whole figure reflected in passing a shop window or caught in a candid snapshot can sometimes be rather a shock.

Given that the time has come to take stock of your assets and of those things which can and should be improved, where do you start? At home, with time to spare, aim to make a cool appraisal that is neither rose-tinted nor deprecating. Do it wearing undies in front of a full-length mirror in a good strong light – and make notes. Examine your figure front and profile. Check the posture of your normal stance when at ease. Note all your good points, the things that need work and those problems which you simply cannot change.

No matter how grim your final list looks you ought to feel encouraged – you have actually begun to do something about it. Forget what you can't change – like your bone structure, the length of your neck or legs. Make up your mind to work on the 'improvables' and approach the task realistically. The degree of effort involved depends on the scope of the problems you want to solve. For instance, losing a lot of weight or correcting serious figure problems requires an energetic long-term programme and patience, whereas adjusting posture can be accomplished in minutes.

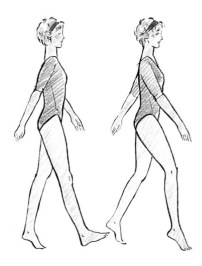

WALKING WELL: Step out on a straight leg. Point your foot directly ahead and come down on your heel, then shift weight to the ball of your foot. Keep head up, arms swinging easily, your step springy and alive.

STANDING TALL: Stand one foot turned out a little, the other a bit ahead. Keep back straight, knees relaxed, hands at your sides. Your tummy and buttocks should be tucked in, your chest up, chin parallel to the floor.

Posture

Like the expression of your eyes or mouth, your carriage is a key to character. Standing and moving well signals self-confidence as well as grace. Are you upstanding, with straight shoulders, pulled-up rib cage, tucked-in tummy, a trim bottom and naturally flexed knees? When you sit down, can you fit both hands – flat, one above the other – between your bosom and your waist? If you can't, you're too crumpled up.

Now stand with your back against a wall, feet about 7.5 cm (3 inches) from it. If your posture is close to perfect, your head, shoulders and buttocks will be touching the wall; the small of your back won't be more than a hand's thickness away. Check your profile in a full-length mirror and drop a pretend plumb line straight down from the top of your head to the bottom of your feet. Does it bisect you at the shoulder, the hip, the knee and the ankle bone? It should. Still not convinced? Try this test: stand normally and measure your waist. Now pull up your rib cage and measure again. Slimmer? Does it seem like magic? It's more like muscles. And muscles must be maintained to make sure you're always standing and moving prettily.

Try to make yourself think about your posture at odd moments throughout the day – play games, as it were. Pretend

8

Sit against wall with legs crossed, arms against wall, bent upward in right angles, all vertebrae touching wall. Slide arms up until straight above your head. Do 10 times.

Lie on the floor with arms over head, knees bent, feet flat on floor. Pull in abdomen so small of back presses against floor; hold, then relax. Do 10 times.

Lie on floor with knees bent, feet flat, arms bent at elbows. Pull in abdomen while you straighten legs and arms. Count to 10, then relax. Do 10 times.

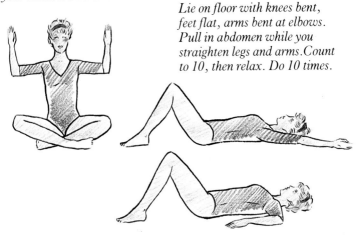

you're a puppet on strings being pulled up, up, up. Try to touch an imaginary ceiling with the top of your head. Make believe your tummy and back are book-ends and squeeze them tightly together. Think of your body as a set of child's building bricks – stack them straight or they'll fall down.

Think about being a jack-in-the-box. Place your hands opposite each other at the back and front of your waist. Tuck down your tail, lift your stomach up and in and you'll find that your hands are no longer parallel. Applaud, as if at the theatre: clap your hands in front, above the head and behind you. Then demand an encore – just think what it's doing for those sagging shoulders – but this time with the hands back to back.

With more time to spare, do a few specific posture exercises. The three shown above are all designed to strengthen back muscles and straighten slumped shoulders and swaybacks (the two most common posture faults). Whether you choose to do one or all three, the secret is daily repetition. Work slowly and rhythmically, stretching until you feel a 'pull'.

Remember that every effort you make to improve your posture and give your movements grace, every 10 minutes you spend exercising for a trim lithe body will bring dividends – in the way your clothes fit and move, in the way you feel about yourself, in the way others see you.

General Fitness

Literally everyone – fat, thin or just right – needs exercise. Not just the muscles you use to climb stairs, load the washing-machine, do the shopping, but all the muscles need their share of activity to stay firm, strong and flexible. Even if you are an active sports fan, only a few sports – swimming, volleyball or fencing – give you muscle tone all over. Ballet and modern dance also do a good job. But if you don't go in for one of these every week of the year, the best guarantee of a complete work-out is daily exercise at home. All the authorities on the subject agree that a 10-minute daily routine is more effective than a sporadic hour-long dose when the mood moves you – though even that is better than nothing. Choose exercises you enjoy. The range is so wide you can assemble a group of exercises that perfectly suit your figure and temperament needs – fast, slow, more vigorous or less.

However unfit you are, the great joy is that even after long under-use or disuse, the muscles will still increase in girth and power if they're exercised properly again. The most important thing is to build up gradually. It's a mistake – and may even be dangerous – to go from complete inactivity to strenuous exercise all at once.

Attitudes to exercise: Choose a time and a place convenient for you. There's no ideal time of the day to exercise, although last thing at night, directly after meals and directly after getting up should be avoided.

Choose a private place unless you're making this a group project. There's something to be said for exercising in the company of a few friends, but any time the others fail to appear you might be tempted to skip the routine. Group exercising works best for weekly work-outs.

The ideal 'gym' is a well-ventilated, heated room – your bedroom is probably the best location. Rearrange furniture if necessary; the area you need for freedom of movement is ideally your height circumference. A full-length mirror enables you to check that your shoulders and face do not tense up. A cool or warm shower beforehand helps to loosen you up. *Never* exercise after a hot bath: this can not only cause an increase in blood pressure but really relaxed muscles can become strained through overdoing things. If you feel any stiffness the day after your first attempt at exercise, add a handful of relaxing bath salts to your bath water and steep in it for a while. Exercise in clothing which does not restrict you at all. The ideal flooring is an exercise mat, rug or folded blanket, which helps prevent bruising and skin irritations.

Make an exercise mat: If your exercise area does not have a rug, make an exercise mat in a colour keyed to your leotard. You'll need a pair of beach towels, a length of thin foam rubber 2.5 cm (1 inch) smaller than the towel all round (to allow for the seams) and 3 giant stud fasteners. Sew the towels together on 3 sides to enclose the foam rubber and use the stud fasteners to close the open end.

Eating Habits

A good well-balanced diet is a basic essential for top-to-toe health and the best way to achieve it is to keep to a regular meal pattern. Three meals a day – breakfast, one main meal and one light meal – should be sufficient to provide a healthy balanced diet. How can you be sure that you are getting all the vitamins and minerals that you need? Most easily by eating a wide variety of foods. There is nothing so potentially damaging both physically and mentally than a rigid and unbalanced diet adhered to for more than a few days.

Foods can be allocated to different groups based on the nutrients they contain. Two average portions of food from each of the following groups every day should provide you with enough of all these nutrients.

Group 1: Meat, poultry, fish, eggs
Group 2: Milk, cheese, yogurt
Group 3: Fruit and vegetables
Group 4: Bread, pasta, cereals
Group 5: Butter, margarine, oils

Vegetarians, particularly those who do not eat food in groups 1 or 2, should include a wide variety of vegetable protein foods instead: pulses – lentils, kidney beans, haricot beans, chick peas, etc – nuts and cereals are particularly good sources. They also contain useful vitamins and minerals.

Of course, every person's needs are slightly different, especially as far as calorie intake is concerned. It is also important to realize that most foods in groups 1 and 2 are sources of fats (Group 5) too – weight-watchers take note!

If you find dieting difficult, make just one or two diet changes. Have a fruit breakfast, use a sweetener instead of sugar, have one starch-free meal a day. Season foods with spices or herbs or tart fruit juices – all add variety. Don't overlook psychological aids either. Eat slowly, chew well and eat from a smaller plate. Take the edge off your hunger before a meal with a snack of bouillon, a heart of lettuce or a spoonful of yogurt. When tempted to eat between meals, sip a glass of iced water or eat a bit of cheese with a stick of celery or a tomato.

Excess weight often means faulty elimination. Check this. One cause is a high starch, low vitamin diet. As far as possible, avoid white bread, white sugar, white polished rice, cakes, sweets, buns and biscuits and have plenty of protein foods, lightly cooked vegetables, salads and fruit.

Another cause is not enough bulk or roughage in the diet. One of the best ways of overcoming this is to take a bran cereal for breakfast. Make sure that you are also taking enough Vitamin B foods. A daily dose of wheatgerm will often cure

constipation. Make sure that you drink enough water; if you are not regular, try drinking 5 glasses a day between meals.

Although it is true that many people gain a few pounds in weight during the winter, there is no need to regard an increase as inevitable. It's important to keep up the intake of Vitamins A and D during the winter: fresh fruits and vegetables are just as important to winter good looks as they are in summer.

Weight is closely related to metabolism, which governs how fast you burn up the calories you take in when you eat. The metabolic rate is faster in some people than in others, which may partly explain why every chocolate you swallow seems to show while your best friend can live on pasta without seeming to gain an ounce! She may also be much more active and/or tense than you are. Slow metabolism is a favourite excuse for excess pounds, but in fact most people have normal metabolism. The rate does change at different ages however. Growth helps raise the body's basic energy expenditure. Adults use less energy per pound than teenagers.

Calories are energy units and it is not until we are either over-weight or under-weight that we need to worry about them. Cutting down on calories does not mean starving but choosing low calorie foods. For example, a lean lamb cutlet provides 100 calories, so does a chocolate cream!

It takes time to break old eating habits, to plan healthy meals or appetizing low-calorie ones. Ideally, let all the family co-operate with you in planning meals two or three days ahead. If you're one of a large family this helps with the shopping and keeps you organized. There is little chance of error if you add up the calories before instead of after you eat. A slim, firm figure is not the only bonus. Add to that clear skin, bright shiny eyes and swinging vibrant hair.

13

Stress

Stress means different things to different people. Most of us would bracket it with some sort of distress: the distress of sitting up night after night studying, fearful of doing badly in an exam; the distress of running a home on a tight budget, having to shop around, getting tired; the distress of being burdened with elderly parents, having to cope with their problems as well as your own. Stress becomes bottled up inside you. Things like traffic jams, long delays in queues, waiting endlessly for the phone to ring all contribute to a feeling of being wound up internally. For most of us these are isolated examples, but when an anxiety endures and develops into prolonged stress then the body simply wears down.

Signs of stress you can quickly recognize include poor sleep, over-eating or drinking, hunched tense posture and repetitive mannerisms like teeth-clenching, nail-biting or pencil-tapping.

Preventatives: Stress can be alleviated by mental discipline, conscious relaxation and the right kind of food. Let's start with those often vague feelings of worry, rather than actual problems, which often make us tense.

Before going to bed, aim to empty your mind of worries. Take paper and pencil and drag them out into the open,

14

writing down every mild nag in your mind. Having written them down, study them carefully. Can you do anything about this one, for example? No? Then take your pencil and strike it out. The very act of putting your pencil through it will get it off your mind. This worry now? You can do something about that! Well, write down just what you can do and resolve to do it on such and such a date. Do this every night, clearing your mind of worried feelings and watch your stress symptoms disappear.

Watch for points of tension and strain. These are usually the shoulders, hands, feet and face. Check the position of the shoulders frequently. We tend to hold them tensely, sometimes pulling them up almost to the ears. Relax them. Do a few shoulder circling movements. Flap the hands loosely from the wrists to relax them. Make sure that when you are sitting, your legs are not wound round each other or the ankles round the legs of the chair. To relieve neck and shoulder tension, try these spot-relaxers:

1. Shrug your shoulders to your ears – one shoulder at a time – and circle forward 6 times, now backwards 6 times.

2. Relax shoulders and gently roll the head to a full circle, first round to the right, then to the left. Repeat 3 times each side.

3. Not an exercise, but sleeping with a Chinese pillow will help alleviate any unusual sleeping angles which contribute to tension in the neck.

Cures: A course of body massage is a very good antidote to stress and the gentle stroking and manipulating of the spine is ideal for relaxing a tense body. A warm bath, containing some pleasant-smelling herb or perfumed bath essence, is another way of relaxing. So is scalp massage – you can massage your own scalp quite easily, working with gentle circular movements from hairline to crown. Hair-brushing with rubber-based bristles is a very relaxing bedtime exercise. A few minutes face massage every night at bedtime is helpful to relax tense muscles, particularly from the area above the nose up to the hairline of the forehead, along the eyebrows, the temples and the area about the eyes.

Increasing your intake of thiamin (Vitamin B_1) may help. Thiamin is found in whole grains, sunflower seeds, chicken, fish roe, sardines, cod, lean beef, liver, pork and kidney.

Relaxing beverages (and sleep inducing!) include the following: peppermint tea, sweetened with a teaspoonful of honey; a glass of hot milk with 9 drops of oil of cloves added; a cup of lime tisane; orange flower water (an old French cure for sleeplessness) – 1 tablespoon orange flower water in a wine glassful of warm water with a lump of sugar; 1 tablespoon honey taken in hot water, with or without the juice of half a lemon.

Shaping up

Body types: First of all get to know your body type. Don't judge yourself on model girl proportions. Your body type holds the key to your scope for improvement. Your figure fits into one of three categories, which can't be altered, but you can certainly aim for better proportions. It is possible to alter the shape of any part of the body. The only unalterables are the length of your bones. But even the spine can be stretched a little, especially if there is bad posture, which could result in 0.5-1 cm (¼-½ inch) difference in height.

Now for the three body types. If you are an *ectomorph*, small framed with narrow shoulders and often even narrower hips, you should aim to be neat-waisted with little obvious muscle or fat. A *mesomorph* with a medium to large frame, ranging from quite square and angular to comfortably rounded, often with broad shoulders, should be mostly muscle and bone with not much obvious fat and a slim line right through waist and hips. An *endomorph*, heavily built but not necessarily large framed, is sturdy through rib cage, waist and hips and usually quite well covered, but ideally has trim muscles and no excess fat.

Capacity for exercise: Your preference and aptitude for certain types of exercise and sport is often dictated by your figure type. Ideally, settle for those you can perform with enjoyment and a sense of achievement. Don't struggle fruitlessly with an exercise form with which you are not physically compatible.

Ectomorphs usually display qualities of endurance and agility and have good body support, all of which links them with such diverse sports as cross-country running and volleyball. In between, of course, that leaves anything from running, jogging, hiking, skiing, badminton and tennis.

Mesomorphs, with a traditionally muscular frame and scope for developing strength, endurance, power and agility, can be good at just about anything they try, be it running or weight training.

Endomorphs don't rate top marks for strength, agility, endurance, power or body strength. Most true endomorphs will happily admit to being less sporty than many of their acquaintance, having long since discovered that they are better working at their own pace. Favourite activities include those which don't necessarily embrace a competitive element. Things like swimming, cycling, archery and bowling are ideal.

Weight: What Should You Weigh

It is a good idea to monitor your weight level. Ideally, weigh yourself once a week, on the same scales, at the same time of day, wearing the same clothes – or nothing at all. If you are fully dressed, including shoes, allow 2.75 kg (6 lb) for the weight of winter clothes, 1.75 kg (4 lb) for summer clothes.

When you are trying to lose weight, it is a temptation to weigh yourself every day, particularly if you have your own bathroom scales – but this is a mistake. Weight does not drop off regularly but in fits and starts, and the daily check might well discourage you. As a rough guide, aim to stay within 2.25 kg (5 lb) of the normal weight for your body type/frame.

From the mid-thirties onwards, metabolism slows down and needs about 100 calories a day fewer than it did 10 years ago. While this might not sound much, an extra 100 calories a day can add up to about 4.5 kg (10 lb) a year! That's how weight creeps on. Admittedly, there are times in a woman's life when there is a tendency to put on weight: adolescence; after having a baby; or at the menopause. These phases need only be temporary.

How do you assess your type of frame or build? You don't know whether you come in the small, medium or large category? The type of frame you have conditions your weight quite considerably. To find out which section you come under, measure your wrist. If it is less than 14 cm (5½ inches) you have a small frame; 14-16 cm (5½-6½ inches) a medium frame; over 16 cm (6½ inches) a large frame. There are always exceptions to this rule, but it is a good general guide.

How do you know when you are fat? Generally, a doctor will say that you are definitely over-weight if your weight is 10-15 per cent more than that indicated for your frame and height. A variation of 5-10 per cent over or under is generally believed to have no effect upon your health.

Don't feel discouraged if your weight doesn't tumble down accommodatingly after days or even weeks on a strict diet, even though on checking your measurements you find that your inches are a little less. There is a simple reason for this: when a fat cell shrinks through lack of nourishment, it leaves a space which fills up with water – water weighs more than fat – hence no noticeable difference may be registered for quite a while on the scales, though clothes seem to fit better.

What should you weigh?
Desirable weight, without clothes, for women aged 25 plus

Height	Small frame	Medium frame	Large frame
ft. ins.	st. lb.	st. lb.	st. lb.
4 10	6 13	7 6	8 2
4 11	7 2	7 9	8 5
5 0	7 5	7 12	8 8
5 1	7 8	8 1	8 11
5 2	7 11	8 5	9 1
5 3	8 0	8 8	9 5
5 4	8 4	8 13	9 9
5 5	8 9	9 3	9 13
5 6	8 11	9 7	10 3
5 7	9 2	9 11	10 6
5 8	9 6	10 1	10 11
5 9	9 10	10 5	11 2
5 10	10 00	10 9	11 6

Measurements: Measuring up to Ideals

Once you start to lose weight, fat accumulation becomes a diminishing problem. In over-weight, fat tends to accumulate initially in the fat depots, sited in the tummy and waistline areas, the top of the thighs and the upper arms. Only in gross obesity does the body store away weight in other areas. It is impossible to say where any individual will lose fat or bulges first; for some it may be from the waistline, for others the thighs.

If you want to embark on a realignment programme, you should allow from 2 to 12 weeks depending on the amount of reshaping you want to accomplish. You should not try to lose more than 750 g (1½ lb) per week unless you are extremely overweight to begin with. Combining diet and exercise you may be able to remove as much as 2.5 cm (1 inch) a month from fleshy areas. Thus if you want to take off 4.5 kg (10 lb), 2.5 cm (1 inch) from your waist and 5 cm (2 inches) from your hips, you should allow about 10 weeks in which to accomplish your goal.

The chart below gives an indication of how long it should take to lose weight on a sensible diet. Set your own target date and work towards it. Remember it is always advisable to check with your doctor if you want to lose more than 2.75 kg (6 lb).

How long does it take to get rid of bulges?		
Your present weight	**Amount you want to lose**	**Maximum time it should take**
Between 8 st.3 lb and 8 st.13 lb	5 lb	4 weeks
	10 lb	8 weeks
Between 8 st.13 lb and 9 st.9 lb	5 lb	3 weeks
	10 lb	6 weeks
	20 lb	12 weeks
Between 9 st.9 lb and 10 st.5 lb	5 lb	2½ weeks
	10 lb	5 weeks
	20 lb	11 weeks
Between 10 st.5 lb and 11 st.11 lb	5 lb	2 weeks
	10 lb	4 weeks
	20 lb	9 weeks

The ideal scale of measurements is as follows: bust and hips should measure the same; waist should be 25 cm (10 inches) smaller than bust; thighs should be about 15 cm (6 inches) less than waist; calves about 15-18 cm (6-7 inches) less than thighs; ankles about 13-15 cm (5-6 inches) less than calves; and upper arms should be double the size of wrists.

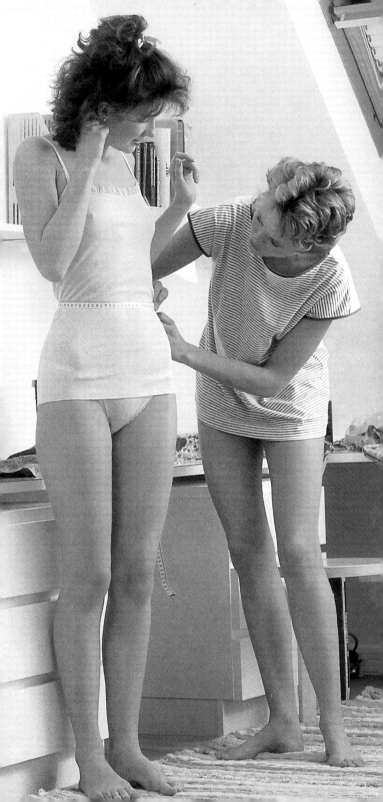

Where to measure: Here are the instructions for taking accurate readings. *Chest:* under armpits, straight around. *Upper arm:* 10 cm (4 inches) down from armpit, then around. *Bust:* straight across back and over the fullest part of the bust. *Waist:* smallest part. *Abdomen:* across the navel, around back, below waist. *Upper hips:* halfway between abdomen and lower hips. *Lower hips:* around the largest part of buttocks. *Top thigh:* up under leg as high as possible, and straight around. *Mid-thigh:* halfway between top thigh measure and knee. *Knee:* around the middle. *Calf:* around the largest part. *Ankle:* around the smallest part, just above ankle bone. Take all measurements with muscles relaxed, and always measure the same limb – right and left limb measurement may be different.

Ideally, measure yourself before you embark on a diet and exercise régime then wait 10 days before taking your measurements again; then another 10 days, and so on.

Always been on the plump side as far back as you can remember? Then double check to see if you are carrying abnormal amounts of body fat. One way of finding out is to lie flat on your back with a ruler on your front. If your weight is normal, the ruler can touch both your ribs and your pelvis. If one end sticks up in the air, it means that something, like fat, is pushing it out.

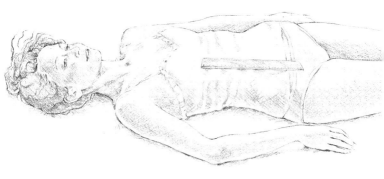

Alternatively, take a deep pinch of skin on your side, just over the lower ribs. If the distance between thumb and index finger is greater than 2.5 cm (1 inch), you are probably too fat. If it is less than 1 cm (½ inch), you are probably too thin. Perfect proportions are, of course, the exception rather than the rule. They should be used as a guide rather than a goal. The best practice is to subtract your ideal measurements from your actual measurements to determine the degree of difference, then strive to cut that difference in half. Thus, if your actual measurements are bust 87 cm (34 inches), waist 66 cm

(26 inches), hips 97 cm (38 inches), and your ideal measurements are bust 87 cm (34 inches), waist 61 cm (24 inches), hips 87 cm (34 inches), your goal would be bust 87 cm (34 inches), waist 64 cm (25 inches) and hips 92 cm (36 inches).

Few of us possess ideal proportions – most of us have at least one main figure fault in need of correction. While diet and exercise are often the answer, they cannot alter bone structure. However, the right choice of clothes for your figure type can give imperfect proportions the illusion of perfection.

Ectomorphs, those with the so-called average figure, are fairly evenly proportioned all over; any silhouette is good on them whether waistlines go up, down or stay put.

The broad-shouldered mesomorph needs emphasis below the waist to balance her light-bulb silhouette. That means keeping major pattern and colour accents below the waist, with everything above under-stated and non-clingy. This figure type looks great in trousers of all lengths.

The sturdy, usually well-rounded endomorph looks best in classic trim shapes with soft, rather than very tailored outlines. Medium length jackets are good for this figure and it pays to keep major accents small in scale most of the time.

23

Exercise

Greater physical fitness is within the grasp of anyone willing to exercise regularly. And it can be fun. So what do we really know about exercise?

It isn't a question of jogging being good or bad, or tennis being better than badminton. What is clear is that any physical activity – any exertion at all – increases your potential for physical ability. And that's what exercise is all about. It doesn't matter whether you can run faster, swim harder or lift heavier weights than the next man, woman or child. It does matter, at any age, if you find it an effort to run the length of the bus stop, to climb the stairs to the top deck, or even to ease yourself out of a sitting position in the evening.

Once you've managed to get over the hurdle of thinking that exercise is a burdensome chore, are beginning to enjoy it and count the blessings of your increased fitness, you're ready to go on to a specific exercise routine. The ideal programme should progress and exercise the body in every way, which means that the programme should include exercises of three different types: for suppleness (mobility); for strength; for stamina (heart and lung exercises).

Mobility exercises persuade the major joints and muscles to move through their complete range of movement. Eventually, as you progress, you will find that you can turn, stretch, twist in every direction with greater freedom and grace.

Male or female, old or young, we all need a certain amount of muscle strength so that we can lift, pull, push or carry heavy objects when necessary. Strength is developed by exercising the limbs and trunk against resistance.

Stamina is dependent on the efficiency of the heart and lungs. To exercise these organs we have to increase the oxygen requirements of the body and this is most easily done by exercising the legs, arms and trunk. This is where running, jogging and ball games come in – and this is where so many people worry about the possibility of heart attack. It's generally advised that no one over fifty, overweight or with a history of heart disease should start any kind of exercise programme without consulting a doctor.

The exercises in this chapter cover the full spectrum. Some are in two stages: beginners and advanced. That way you can learn an exercise efficiently and then go on to develop its full potential. Do not be in a hurry to progress – wait until you can do the full number of repetitions comfortably at the first level.

General Exercise Plan

TOE TOUCH FOR BEGINNERS:
Stand erect, feet slightly apart,
hands over head. Bend forward
from waist to touch toes with
fingertips. Keep knees straight
even if you can't reach toes at
first. Return to standing
position before repeating. Begin
with 20, gradually speed up
to 40.

TOE TOUCH, ADVANCED PLAN:
Stand erect, feet about 40 cm
(16 inches) apart, toes pointed
out, arms extended straight out
from shoulders. Keep arms
straight and bend from waist to
touch left foot with right hand.
Do not bend knees. Return to
starting position, then repeat on
other side, touching right foot
with left hand. Begin with 15,
gradually increase to 25.

BENDS FOR BEGINNERS: Stand erect, feet about 30 cm (12 inches) apart, hands clasped together over head. Bend from the waist to right side, keeping back straight and arms extended. Return to starting position, then bend to other side. Continue, alternating sides. Begin with 10 on each side, increase to 20.

ADVANCED BENDS: Stand erect, feet 30 cm (12 inches) apart, arms extended. Bend right arm over head, dropping left arm to side. Keep back straight and bend from waist. Slide left arm down leg as far as possible. Return to start and repeat on other side. Begin with 10 each side, increase to 20.

KNEES BEND: Stand erect, feet together, arms forward, Rise upon toes, then slowly bend knees. Keep back straight and arms extended. Return to start at same speed. Begin with 10, work up to 20.

27

ARM SWING FOR BEGINNERS:
Stand erect, feet together, arms
extended in front with hands
about waist level. Swing arms
around and as far back as they
will go, then swing forward to
starting position. Begin with
25, gradually increasing speed
to 50.

ARM SWING, ADVANCED PLAN:
Stand erect, feet together, arms
extended straight forward at
shoulder level. Keeping arms
straight, swing them around
and as far back as they will go.
Keep arms at shoulder level and
swing back to starting position.
Begin with 40, increase to 60.

HIP ROLL: Lie flat on back, legs
together, arms extended from
shoulders, palms down. Keep
legs together and tuck up close to
chest. Keeping knees together
and shoulders on floor, roll over

to left side until left leg is flat on
floor. Keeping legs tucked up,
roll back until right leg is flat on
floor. Begin by touching each
leg to the floor 10 times, work
up to 25 each side.

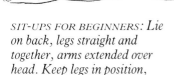

SIT-UPS FOR BEGINNERS: Lie on back, legs straight and together, arms extended over head. Keep legs in position, back as straight as possible and move to a sitting position. Bend from the waist to touch toes with hands. Return at same speed to starting position. Begin with 10, work up to 25.

SIT-UPS, ADVANCED PLAN: Lie on back, legs straight and together, hands clasped behind head. Keep legs in position, back as straight as possible and move to sitting position. Bend forward with head down. Return at same speed to starting position. Hold abdomen in throughout. Start with 20, work up to 35.

29

LEG SWING: Stand erect, feet together, left hand on wall for support, right hand at side. Keeping back and legs straight, swing right leg up, then down and back. Point toes and reach as high as possible. Swing 10 times. Reverse position and repeat with left leg. Work up to 20.

LEG KICK: Lie on side, legs straight, head on extended lower arm. Use other arm for balance. Keeping legs straight, raise upper leg until perpendicular to floor, then lower to start position. Begin with 10 each leg, work up to 20.

RUNNING ON SPOT: Stand erect, feet together, hands on hips. Run on spot, raising knees higher and increasing speed as you go.

PUSH-UPS FOR BEGINNERS:
Lie face down, legs together,
forearms along floor with
elbows directly under shoulders.
Raise body from the floor by
straightening back. Balance on
toes and elbows. Lower body
back to floor and repeat without
resting in between. Begin with
5, gradually work up to 15.

PUSH-UPS, ADVANCED PLAN:
Lie face down, legs straight and
together, hands flat and
pointing forward directly under
shoulders. Push body up from
hands and toes until arms are
fully extended. Keep body and
legs in straight line and lower by
bending elbows. Touch chest to
floor and repeat without resting.
Begin with 3, gradually work
up to 10.

Eliminating Figure Faults

The exercises on the following pages are designed to correct common figure problems in 10 areas of the body:

Bustline: Exercise will strengthen the muscles which support your bust. It won't add much to the size, but it will firm and uplift, giving you a prettier contour. The same exercises will also make your bust seem larger by correcting shoulder slump.

Upper arms: The muscles in the upper arms are among the most neglected in a woman's body. Exercise is essential to prevent and correct flabbiness.

Midriff: Exercise combined with good posture will quickly flatten and firm this area while increasing its flexibility.

Waistline: Exercise works wonders in whittling away excess inches in this crucial area.

Abdomen: The key to a flat tummy is strong abdominal muscles, which are readily attained with persistent exercise.

Bottom: Exercise reduces the fat in this area and strengthens the muscles which control firmness.

Hips: There are many exercises which will reduce and firm the flesh in this area, even without loss of weight.

Thighs: Persistent exercise will turn flabbiness into firmness while slowly whittling off an inch or two.

Calves: The same exercises that slim down heavy calves will also add pretty curves to thin ones.

Ankles: Exercise cannot perform miracles but it can trim as much as 2-3 cm (1 inch) off your ankles. It also tones and strengthens the muscles.

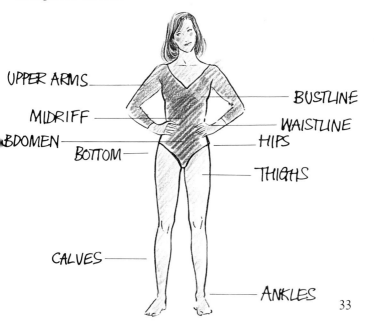

UPPER ARMS

MIDRIFF

BDOMEN

BOTTOM

BUSTLINE

WAISTLINE

HIPS

THIGHS

CALVES

ANKLES

33

Bust

Stand erect, feet together, arms at sides. Hold weights in each hand (such as full soft drink bottles or polythene containers of salt or vinegar). Lift hands over head, then swing back down and around to form a complete circle with each hand. Begin with 10 circles, work up to 20.

Stand erect, elbows bent, fingertips touching in front of chin. Keep arms at shoulder level and pull elbows back as far as they go. Return to start and repeat. Begin with 5, work up to 15.

Upper Arms

Lie down, legs together, arms at sides, hands holding weights (such as full soft drink bottles or polythene containers full of salt). Keeping arms straight, lift weights until arms are fully extended above your head. Slowly lower hands to shoulders, then return to starting position. Begin with 10, work up to 20.

Stand erect, feet apart, hands clasped behind back. Keeping back and arms straight, lift hands as high as you can. Return to start, relax and repeat. Begin with 5, work up to 10.

Midriff

Sit on the floor with legs straight, feet as far apart as possible. Lift left arm over your head and bend to touch right foot with right hand. Return to starting position, then bend to the left. Begin with 5 bends in each direction, work up to 10.

Lie down with knees pulled up to chest, arms at sides. Lift legs straight up, then back over head, using hands to support hips. Return to starting position and repeat. Begin with 5, work up to 10.

Waistline

Stand erect, feet together, arms extended over head. Keep legs straight and bend from waist to touch toes. Return to starting position, then bend back from the waist. Begin with 10, work up to 25.

Sit on floor with legs straight and feet as far apart as possible, hands clasped behind head. Twist to touch right knee with left elbow. Return to starting position, then touch left knee with right elbow. Begin with 5 twists each side, work up to 10.

Abdomen

Lie on floor, legs together, hands clasped under head. Keeping toes pointed and knees straight, lift legs very slowly until pointing to the ceiling. Lower them back into position equally slowly, contracting abdominal muscles as you do so. Begin with 3, work up to 10.

Lie face down, legs together, arms straight at sides. Keeping your legs straight and together, and your toes pointed, lift shoulders and feet from the floor simultaneously so that your body forms an arc. Begin with 5, gradually work up to 10.

Bottom

Lie on floor, arms outstretched from shoulders, palms down. Bend knees, pulling feet as close to buttocks as possible. Contract bottom muscles and press hips upwards into thighs, raising lower back off the floor. Hold for a count of 5, then drop quickly back to starting position. Begin with 5, work up to 15.

Sit Indian-fashion, with soles of feet together, hands on ankles. Keep your back straight and rock from side to side. Begin with 10 rocks to each side, work up to 20.

Hips

Lie down, legs straight, arms at sides, palms down. Point toes and lift legs as high as possible, then slowly move them up and *down alternately in a bicycle motion. Support hips with your hands if necessary. Begin with 15 complete circles, work up to 25.*

Lie down, knees bent, feet on floor, arms extended from the shoulders, palms downwards. Keeping shoulders flat on the floor and knees together, *roll legs rapidly to slap floor on the right, reversing to slap floor on the left. Begin with 10 rolls to each side, work up to 20.*

Thighs

Lie on floor, legs straight, arms at sides, palms down. Lift both legs about 25 cm (10 inches) from the floor, then swing them apart as wide as possible. Swing together, then apart 3 more times before returning to starting position. Begin with 5, work up to 10.

Sit with knees bent, hands and feet resting on floor, as close to your body as possible. Lift up your hips, moving them forward until your knees touch the floor. Return to starting position. Begin with 5, gradually working up to 10.

41

Calves

Stand erect, feet 40 cm (16 inches) apart, right foot turned to side, hands on hips. Lower body to floor, bending right knee, keeping left leg straight. Bob up and down several times, then return to starting position. Repeat on left side. Begin with 5 on each side, work up to 10.

Stand erect, feet together, hands on hips. Lift right knee until thigh is perpendicular to body. With toes pointed, rotate lower leg from knee to draw a circle. Make 5 circles in each direction before returning to starting position. Repeat with left leg. Begin with 3 for each leg, work up to 8.

Ankles

Stand erect, hands on hips, feet together, toes resting on a large book, heels on floor. Lift heels from the floor until you are balancing on toes on edge of book. Begin with 5, work up to 10.

Lie down, legs straight, arms at sides, palms down. Lift right leg about 25 cm (10 inches) from floor and rotate foot from ankle, making a big circle with your big toe. Make 5 circles in each direction, then repeat with left foot. Do 3 or 4 times each side.

43

Daily Dozen

You don't need access to a gym, elaborate equipment or a figure-hugging leotard in order to exercise. There are many excellent exercises you can do at any stage in the day while sitting at your desk or working around the house. Some of these exercises are explained on the following pages. Develop the 'exercise break' habit, for a minute here and a minute there soon add up to a slimmer, trimmer figure.

For instance, aim to bend from your waist or knees instead of stooping, for proper movement is essential to good posture. Deep breathing is excellent for slimming abdomen, increasing flexibility and eliminating fatigue. When you're sitting, simple contraction of abdomen and buttocks is one of the best possible exercises for flattening and firming both areas. One way of keeping the body supple and flexible is to stretch when reaching for objects which are almost – but not quite – out of reach.

At home: When you wash dishes or peel vegetables, don't hunch over the sink: stand upright in an easy relaxed position.

When you brush your teeth, pull in your tummy muscles as if trying to touch them to your spine. Breathing quite normally, hold them there until you have finished brushing.

As you go through a door, stretch up your right hand as if trying to reach the doorway top. Then try to touch it with your left hand. This stretches and slims waist and diaphragm.

Give some thought to heel height. The lower the heel, the better legs are exercised naturally, but as each heel height exercises muscles others don't – vary your shoes.

When sitting, tighten the abdominal and buttock muscles. Hold as long as you can, relax, then repeat.

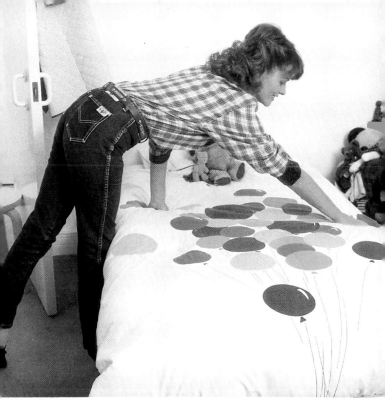

ABOVE: When making beds, bend from the waist and stretch your body across the width of the bed. Keep your back as straight as possible when performing all such household chores.

LEFT: Stand in front of an open window and breathe deeply, rising up on your toes and flinging your arms wide. Exhale, relax and repeat 5 times.

RIGHT: Never use a footstool or ladder unless absolutely necessary. Stretch your body from head to toe when reaching for out-of-the-way objects.

Every time you bend, perform an exercise. Standing up and bending from the waist exercises muscles in the backs of the legs and slims the waistline. Sitting down and bending over to the floor at the side is excellent for slimming waist and midriff. Another way to pick up something from the floor is to stand near the object and kneel on one knee before picking it up. As you rise, use your thigh muscles not the muscles of your back. This helps to keep slender thighs and prevent back strain.

Don't forget about exercising in bed or in the bath. In the bath, for instance, you can slim waist and diaphragm by keeping the legs straight and touching left foot with right hand and right foot with left hand. When drying yourself, take the towel and hold it near the centre with both hands. With bent elbows, swing arms to right at shoulder level and wring towel hard. Swing to left and wring again. Good for firming the bust.

Worried about a double chin? Before you get up in the morning, lie on your back, head extended over the edge of your bed. Let your head drop backwards, then raise it up and forwards onto your chest.

For a firm bosom, lie on top of your bed with the upper part of your body supported and make strong swimming motions with your arms. Or clench your fists and tuck them into your armpits, then make circles with your elbows as if trying to fly.

Pick up non-heavy objects from the floor by bending from the waist, keeping your legs straight; this exercises muscles in backs of legs and slims the waistline.

An alternative way of picking up objects from the floor is to sit on a straight chair or stool and bend over to the side, keeping your back straight; excellent for slimming waist and midriff.

At the office: An exercise to strengthen upper arm and chest muscles is shown above: Prop your right elbow on the desk and balance a heavy book on your fingertips. Lift the book up until the arm is fully extended above your head. Lower and repeat 5 times, then switch the book to the other hand.

Here are 2 good leg exercises. Sit on a desk or table and bend the right foot upwards from the ankle as far as it will go, then downwards. Repeat this with the left foot and finally with both feet together. Alternatively, place a telephone book at your feet. Slipping off your shoes, put one foot on the book, the foot turned slightly inwards, toes hanging over the edge. Then stretch toes down towards the floor but keep heel flat on book.

Do a few facial exercises. To help alleviate vertical frown lines, pull your eyebrows way down over your eyes. In other words, frown so hard it feels as though you were trying to get your eyebrows to meet each other end on. Then lift your eyebrows as high – and open your eyes as wide – as you can.

To help tone upper eyelids, open your mouth slightly, raise your eyebrows and close your eyes. As you raise your eyebrows up, stretch forward with your eyelids. Feel as if you're trying to get the greatest possible distance between your eyebrows and lashes. Hold for a count of 10. Very slowly and consciously, relax the eyelids, returning eyebrows to normal position.

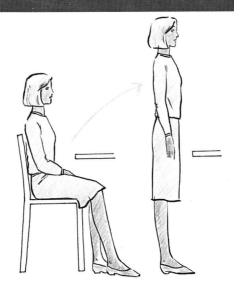

Sit erectly with your back straight, feet flat on the floor, right foot slightly forward, hands in your lap. Rise to a standing position using only your leg muscles. Lower yourself

slowly back into position. Repeat when you have occasion to get in or out of your seat. This movement strengthens leg muscles and helps slim calves and thighs.

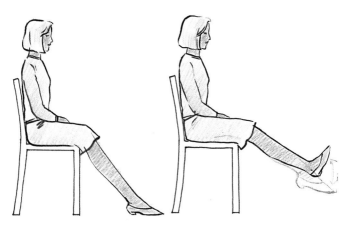

Stretch your legs out in front of you with toes pointed. Lift both feet up about 30 cm (12 inches) from the floor. Keeping knees together and legs straight, move

your feet rapidly up and down scissor-fashion. This stimulates leg circulation and strengthens muscles.

48

Place both hands on your desk, palms down, fingers together, elbows bent. Press down in an effort to lift your body slightly from the chair. Hold pressure for a few seconds, then relax. This tones and strengthens muscles of the shoulders and upper arms.

Rotate your head in a wide circle from the base of your neck. Begin with 2 circles, work up to 5. This tones the neck muscles and helps to keep chin and neck firm.

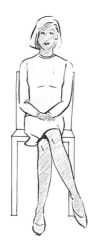

Cross your legs, right over left, with toes pointed. Rotate your right foot from the ankle as if you were drawing a wide circle with your big toe. Make

5 circles in each direction, then repeat with your left foot. An excellent exercise for strengthening and slimming the ankles.

49

Good Sports

Outdoor activities like tennis, skiing and swimming are excellent forms of exercise. Indoor movements which stimulate the muscles used in these sports are good fun and help achieve better results when you come to do the real thing. Apart from anything else, they build up confidence and an awareness of the joints and muscles that are most in play.

The tennis routine is designed to keep joints mobile, muscles flexible, and eye and foot control co-ordinated. A pre-ski programme should ideally start several months before you set off for the slopes. Running, jogging, jumping and skipping, climbing stairs, learning to balance on one leg will all help prepare the body for the rigours of the ski scene. Although there is no need to be fit to enjoy a swim, power and efficiency in the water can be greatly enhanced by exercising on dry land.

So when the weather goes against you, don't despair: keep in trim with an indoor routine. And when the sun shines or the snow is right and you're going to do the real thing, these basic exercises are particularly effective as warm-ups.

Tennis routine

Stand erect, feet 15 cm (6 inches) apart, hands clasped together behind back. Keeping back and arms straight, lift hands as high as you can. Return to start. Begin with 5, work up to 10.

Stand erect, feet about 30 cm (12 inches) apart, hands clasped together over head. Bend from the waist to right side, keeping back straight and arms extended. Return to starting position, then bend to other side. 10 on each side.

Sit on floor, hugging head to knees, arms clasped round legs, feet together. Holding position, rock backwards, until back touches floor. Rock back and forth gently 8 to 10 times.

Skiing routine

Stand erect, arms by your sides. Keeping feet flat on floor, raise arms as high as you can for a count of 5. Lower them slowly.

Stand with arms raised above head and, moving from waist up, swing arms as far to the left as possible, then to the right. Do 4 times.

Stand erect with your arms raised at the sides to shoulder level. Swing arms back as far as you can. Then swing them forward. Repeat up to 6 times.

Stand erect, feet together, arms raised behind you, palms up. Bend knees as far as you can; keep upper body straight. Slowly straighten up. Repeat 4 times.

Stand erect, feet together. Keeping body straight and feet flat on floor, bend knees, twisting them to the left. Straighten and twist to the right. Repeat 4 times.

Stand erect, feet together, right heel against a sturdy chair leg. Bend knees and swing to right, aiming to clasp chair leg with left hand. Do 4 times each side.

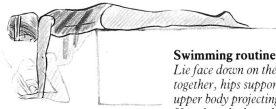

Swimming routine

Lie face down on the bed, feet together, hips supported by bed, upper body projecting over side. Keep legs, body and head straight. Gradually lower body until elbows and forehead touch floor. Slowly straighten arms and raise head and body to starting position. Repeat 3 to 4 times.

Lie flat on your back and, keeping legs together, bring your knees up over your chest – as far as you can. Clasp hands over ankles and try to touch knees with forehead. Slowly straighten legs to lie flat again. Repeat 2 to 3 times.

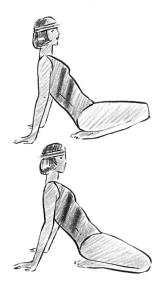

Sit on the floor with knees bent and feet tucked under buttocks. With hands on floor behind you, lean back, raising your knees to stretch ankles. Repeat 5 times.

Stand with your arms raised to shoulder height in front of you, palms together. Keeping arms at shoulder level, pull them back hard to sides. Repeat 5 times.

53

Pregnancy

Even if the idea of exercising is your pet aversion, overcome it during pregnancy: your figure and general health will benefit enormously and with muscles in good strong condition, no special maternity underpinnings should be necessary. Most doctors agree that plenty of fresh air and exercise are important for good general health and to keep muscles in fine tone. But violent exercise is best avoided, especially during the last few months, and don't, at any time, go lugging at – or trying to lift – heavy objects.

The healthy way is to carry on with normal daily work but to do as much of it as possible sitting down – and miss no opportunity of putting your feet up. Aim to do one or two foot exercises every day, if only to encourage you to sit down. For instance, with your heels resting on the floor, bend your feet upward from the ankle. Bend your feet down again. Repeat often during the day. Or, with your heels resting on the floor, curl up your toes tightly, straighten out and repeat.

It is extremely good for women in the later stages of pregnancy to spend some time each day relaxing with their feet up. Raising the feet higher than the hips relieves pressure on the pelvic veins, aids circulation in the legs and helps to prevent varicose veins and swollen ankles. Pain in the tail bone

is quite common during pregnancy, depending on the extra weight involved. Try placing a cushion under your thighs for relief when sitting.

Eating correctly ensures that you do not put on unnecessary weight, and correct posture and gentle controlled exercise ensure that after the baby is born the body returns quickly and easily to its former shape.

Once your doctor or midwife has given you the go-head to start working your way back to your normal weight and shape, limber up every day – on waking – by stretching every part of your anatomy.

Still lying in bed, on a hard mattress if possible, bend your right knee up to your chin, holding it there with your hands. Slowly lift head, neck and shoulders up as you pull your knee closer and closer. Hold for a count of 5, then relax as you lower your head back down. Repeat with the left leg.

Lie on your back with your legs out straight. Keeping your heels on the bed, make small circling movements with your feet, first inwards, then outwards.

Lie on your back with both knees raised and your feet flat on the bed. Pull in the muscles of your abdomen and slowly roll your knees over to the right, then back up again. Repeat, rolling to the left.

Before: Good posture is vital during pregnancy; the hollow backward-leaning stance is one of the most common causes of backache in pregnant women. Also, it is important to learn to contract the pelvic floor muscles if their elasticity is to be retained after the birth. General exercises are also valuable.

Lie on your back with knees bent and feet flat. Breathing normally, tighten your buttock muscles by squeezing the two sides of your bottom together

and, at the same time, pull in your abdominal muscles to feel the hollow of your back press against floor. Hold for 5 seconds, then relax. Do 5 times slowly.

Kneel on all fours with knees directly below your hips and your hands directly below your shoulders. Slowly arch your

back and draw in your pelvis, tucking in your seat. Hold this arched position for 5 seconds, then relax. Repeat 6 to 8 times.

Lie on your back with your knees bent and your feet flat. Straighten your left knee to

extend your leg along the floor. Repeat with right leg. Repeat 5 to 10 times with each leg.

After: During pregnancy, muscles in the abdomen, pelvic region and rib cage become stretched, and often, as physical activities are restricted, other muscles of the body lose their tone. These exercises are designed to strengthen the stretched – as well as the little-used – muscles and to help get the organs in the abdominal cavity back into position. Always ask your doctor's advice about when to start exercising and which exercises you should tackle: 6 to 10 days after the birth is usually about right. Do the following exercises daily.

Lie on your back with knees bent, feet flat and hands on thighs. Pulling in your abdominal muscles and raising your head and shoulders

slightly, slide your hands slowly along your thighs towards your knees. Slowly slide your hands back again and lie flat. Repeat 10 to 12 times, working up to 24.

Lie on your back with knees bent and feet flat. Place arms out to the sides with elbows straight and hands at hip level, palms up. With arms straight,

reach over with your left hand to touch your right hand, raising your head to look at your hands. Repeat on other side. Repeat 5 times, working up to 24.

Sleep & relaxation

How to relax, how to let yourself go – even if it is just for a few minutes every day or for a good night's sleep – is a secret well worth knowing. It really doesn't matter how busy you are at home with your household chores and children, or at work with a profession, learning to relax and being able to enjoy sound sleep are the secrets of peace of mind and happiness.

Sleep

A minimum of 8 hours sleep each night is a necessity for beauty, and an extra bonus of sleep each night will often improve the looks as much as a holiday. When eyes are tired, the complexion drab and the spirits low, the cure can often be found in sleep, but the sleep must be sound sleep: it must have quality as well as quantity.

To ensure sound sleep, the room must be quiet, dark and airy. The mattress must be smooth and straight, firm but resilient, the pillows neither too soft nor too hard, and the bedclothes warm but light.

If you sleep badly, check for constipation or indigestion. It is said that insomnia is often due to mild indigestion caused by a heavy or indigestible meal taken too near bedtime, or to some barely noticeable acidity. Try making the last meal of the day light and digestible, substituting a cup of peppermint tea or lime tisane for the possibly too stimulating tea or coffee.

Most cases of insomnia will react favourably to a warm bedtime bath. An excellent go-to-sleep bath is as follows: Use hot but not too hot water to which you have added a measure of pine-needle oil. Relax in the bath, dry slowly and without effort, then have a soothing drink and go straight to bed.

When you go to bed, think about relaxing rather than about sleeping and, in fact, refuse to let yourself go to sleep until every muscle in your body is completely relaxed. If you find this difficult, do a few relaxing exercises before your drink.

When the whole of your body is as relaxed as you can get it, it will begin to feel heavy and you won't want to move. That's fine – at bedtime! At other times, you may feel so comfortable and lethargic that you will want to drop off to sleep. If you have to get up and get going with other tasks and activities, be warned: your body is now working at a lower level, so take your time to return to normal. Never jump up quickly from relaxation – you might feel giddy. Clench and unclench your fists several times before you sit up, and sit up before you stand.

Relaxation

With practice, you can indulge yourself in a relaxation treatment whenever you like. You can do it lying on the floor or on the bed, or even sitting in a chair, although it does help if you can lie down. Stretch yourself out, close your eyes, let yourself go, and relax from your toes right up to the scalp and hair. Don't think of anything except your relaxing body. Relax your toes, feet, ankles, calves, knees, thighs and gradually, in your thoughts, come slowly up and up through your body until you reach the tips of your fingers, and lastly your hair. Keep going over in your mind – from feet to legs, from fingers to arms and then, lastly and most important, to face, scalp and hair.

If you have time to relax further, start to concentrate on your weight on the floor: feel the heels pressing hard on the ground – suddenly you feel your legs are like lead – then slowly the upper part of the body, the arms and the head, all feel heavy.

Still with eyes closed, concentrate on breathing in slowly through your nose and out through your mouth. Keep on breathing in and out very slowly until you feel that you are starting to float in the air, like a cloud floating in the sky.

Try to spare 10 to 15 minutes a day for this kind of mental exercise for your mind and body. You will feel wonderfully relaxed and content and your nervous system and body will have a new vitality.

When we deliberately relax our muscles, many other changes follow naturally. Blood pressure drops, heart beat and breathing slow down. The only trouble is that it isn't easy to learn to relax all the muscles in the body completely, and at will. Most people find it much easier to relax if they can lie in a really comfortable position, like one of the three illustrated on the opposite page.

You'll probably need a heap of pillows under your head and shoulders, and one for your knees. If you're skinny, you might need support under your elbows too. Experiment until you have found which position is best for you, wear loose comfortable clothing, and remove any hair accessories or chunky jewellery.

You must accept the fact that a woman's work is never done, not try to prove it false. You may be doing unnecessary jobs – never finding time to relax – because you have created rules you won't break. Monday is washing day, but one Monday you feel washed-out. Do you switch your timetable? All too often you struggle on with the chores and find that you are completely exhausted and miserable at the end of the day. Better to miss out and 'put your feet up' for a couple of hours – you will feel much better in the long run.

Lie on your right side. Extend your right leg and bend your left knee up. Bend your left arm so that your hand is on a level with your face, and relax your right arm behind you, palm up. Close your eyes and relax.

To rest and relieve aching or tired leg muscles and feet, lie for a few minutes with your feet on a pillow or book, to raise them slightly above your head.

Lie flat on your back with your arms by your sides, palms up. Let your arms and legs go limp and allow your feet to fall gently apart. Raise your chin, close your eyes and breathe deeply and regularly.

61

Yoga

It's easy to think of yoga, with its Indian origins, as a form of religion but that is not necessarily the case. Physical or Hatha Yoga is a series of well thought-through postures or poses that can benefit almost every part of the body. Not least of the merits of yoga are the relaxing properties. Many a woman under pressure would let everything else go by the board – lunch with a girl friend, a hair appointment, a shopping spree – rather than miss out on her yoga class.

Ideally, for the best possible introduction to yoga, go to a class; simple poses, however, can be practised at home. It is important to do each movement slowly and smoothly, and a good deal of practice is needed before some of the advanced poses can be attempted.

You should breathe slowly and deeply through the nose while doing yoga. Performing the movements correctly is priority: more detailed breathing instructions come into play when you are more advanced. Whether you practise for a few minutes or half an hour, concentrate completely on what you are doing. Shut out sounds, any distraction whatsoever.

One of the most relaxing exercises is to flop like a rag doll. Stand with your feet apart, arms at your sides. With your head and arms hanging, let your body bend forward as far as it will go. Count to 10, then slowly straighten up. With practice, your body will bend until your hands touch the floor. This exercise relaxes the head, neck, shoulders, arms, hands and back, and gently stretches the lower back and backs of the legs. Also, blood can flow to the head and this has a very refreshing effect.

Rolling the head is another very relaxing exercise which helps reduce tension in the neck and is very soothing to do. To avoid headaches and tensions, it is essential to keep the muscles and bones of the neck lubricated and free of settling toxins and poisons. You can do this exercise standing, but it's easier when sitting down, either on a chair or cross-legged on the floor. Do not attempt the Lotus position shown in the picture opposite: a good deal of practice will be necessary before you are able to hold this pose. For the time being, just sit with the legs comfortably crossed.

Head rolling: With eyes looking straight ahead, turn head to the left and hold for a couple of seconds. Roll the head round to the back and hold. Then roll the head around to the right and hold, before turning the face completely to the right with the chin raised. Drop the head forward, letting it feel heavy – be aware of the muscle pull on each side of the neck. Gently push the head down as you bring it round to the front again. Repeat once or twice in each direction.

To show how yoga can let you extend yourself without strain, here is an exercise which stretches and elongates the sides of the body, firming the torso as well as the legs and arms.

Stand with your feet well apart and your arms stretched sideways from the shoulders. Slowly bend to the left from your hips, keeping your right arm in line with your shoulder and holding your left knee with your left hand – both arms should be straight. Bring your right arm over, still straight and as close to your head as possible, and hold for a count of 5. Repeat on the other side. As you repeat this exercise, you will find that you can bring your arm over a little further until, eventually, it is parallel to the floor. You will be able to bend the supporting elbow so the body is brought over still further from the hips.

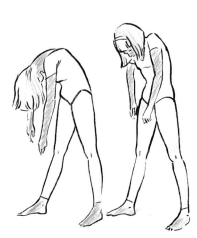

Stand with your feet apart, arms at your sides. With your head and arms hanging, let your body bend forward as far as it will go. Count to 10, then slowly straighten up. With practice, your body will bend until your hands touch the floor.

With eyes looking straight ahead, turn head to left. Hold for a couple of seconds. Roll the head round to the back and hold. Roll to the right and hold, before turning face completely to the right with the chin raised. Drop the head forward, letting it feel heavy, then gently push head down as you bring it round to the front again. Repeat in the opposite direction.

Stand with feet well apart, arms stretched sideways from the shoulders. Slowly bend to the left from the hips, keeping right arm in line with the shoulder and holding left knee with left hand – both arms should be straight. Bring right arm over, still straight and as close to the head as possible. Hold for a count of 5. Repeat on other side.

65

Healthy eating

To maintain good health a well balanced diet is essential; i.e. one that provides adequate amounts of proteins, vitamins and minerals with the correct energy requirement – calories.

Each person varies in their requirements of nutrients and energy, and these change during their lifetime, i.e. during growth, pregnancy and breast feeding, and in old age. If certain nutrient needs are not met, this may lead to minor ailments, such as lethargy and poor complexion, whilst greater deficiency can lead to more serious illnesses, such as anaemia. Excess of certain foods can also be detrimental to health.

The Main Nutrients

Proteins: These provide the materials (amino acids) which are required for growth and repair of body cells. Some of the amino acids are classed as essential in that they cannot be produced in the body so have to be included in the diet. If there is an excessive intake of protein or a lack of calories, protein is broken down to provide energy. Protein can be provided by animal products, such as meat, fish, milk, eggs and cheese, and/or plant materials – cereals, nuts, beans, pulses and vegetables. Animal sources contain all the essential amino acids whereas plant materials may have one or more essential amino acids missing. This is overcome in vegetarian diets by mixing nuts, pulses and cereals so that the amino acids become balanced.

Fats: These provide a concentrated form of energy, i.e. they provide 9 calories/gm compared to proteins and carbohydrates which supply 4 calories/gm. Our diet consists of visible fats, such as butter, margarine, cooking fats, oils and fat on meat, and invisible fats, such as those in cakes, biscuits, nuts and lean meat.

Carbohydrates: These are also used to provide energy, and can be divided into:

Sugars – those naturally occurring in fruit, vegetables, plants and honey, and those that are refined into a concentrated form, such as table sugar, syrup, etc.

Starches – present in potatoes, bread, flour, cereal products, rice, pasta, etc. Starch is not as readily digestible as sugars but cooking makes it more so.

Cellulose and related substances – these form the fibrous structure of the cell walls of plants and are mostly indigestible

even after cooking. The fibrous bulk is essential in the diet for bowel functioning.

Vitamins: These are only required by the body in very small amounts. There are two groups of vitamins – fat soluble (A, D, E and K) and water soluble (B group and C). The fat soluble vitamins can be stored in the body whereas water soluble vitamins cannot and therefore have to be eaten every day.

Vitamin A – essential for vision in dim light, healthy skin and surface tissue. It is only found naturally in animal foods – especially liver, kidney, dairy produce and oily fish. The body can also obtain Vitamin A from carotene which is found in yellow and green vegetables. Another source is margarine which is fortified with vitamin A. Excessive intake of this vitamin is toxic.

Vitamin D – necessary for absorption of calcium and maintaining its level in the blood. Deficiency can lead to deficiency in calcium and hence rickets. Excessive intake can cause deposits of calcium in the kidneys (stones). Vitamin D can be produced by the action of sunlight on certain substances in the skin so dietary needs are small, except during pregnancy and lactation or if a person has little exposure to the sun. Dietary sources are oily fish, butter, and margarine which is enriched.

Vitamin E – the function of this is not fully understood but it is widespread in foods and a deficiency is unlikely.

Vitamin B group – these vitamins are required for the utilisation of energy.

Thiamin (B_1) – widely distributed in foods, rich sources being milk, offal, pork, eggs, vegetables, fruit, wholegrain cereals and fortified breakfast cereals.

Riboflavin (B_2) – widely distributed in foods. The main source in the UK being milk.

Nicotinic acid – there are many sources, the main ones being meat, fish, cheese and bread.

B_6 – used for the metabolism of amino acids. Occurs in meats, fish, eggs and wholegrain cereals.

B_{12} – needed for the production of blood and found only in animal foods, especially liver.

Folic acid – also needed for blood formation. Sources include offal, raw green leafy vegetables, pulses, bread, oranges.

Vitamin C – essential for healthy tissues. The main sources of vitamin C are fruit and vegetables. Care has to be taken because it is easily lost during storage, preparation and cooking.

Minerals: These control many bodily functions. Iron, calcium, phosphorus, magnesium, sodium, chlorine and potassium are the major minerals; others, such as fluoride, are required but only in trace amounts.

Iron – essential for blood. Deficiency causes anaemia. Sources in the diet include meat, especially offal, egs and vegetables.

Calcium – for bones, teeth and muscles. Sources in the diet are cheese, milk, bread and flour (which are fortified), and green vegetables.

Phosphorus – abundant in the body, and present in most foods.

Magnesium – in bones and all body cells. Widespread in food, especially vegetables.

Sodium and Chlorine – in all body fluids with the main source being salt. Usually consumed in excess of need.

Potassium – in body fluids. Sources include vegetables, fruit, meat and milk.

A Healthier Diet

Although malnutrition is quite rare in this country, problems arising from excesses of food are not and a large proportion of the population is overweight. Many diseases, such as diabetes, heart disease, high blood pressure and gall stones, are linked with overweight. For a healthier diet try to adapt your eating pattern as follows:

● Consume less fat – from both visible (butter, margarine, fats and oils, fat on meat) and invisible (cakes, biscuits, fried foods) sources. Obtain fat from vegetable sources rather than animal so that polyunsaturated fatty acid intake is increased at the expense of saturated fatty acids. Fat intake affects the cholesterol and lipoprotein levels in the blood which have been implicated with coronary heart disease.

● Eat less sugar – sugar is a carbohydrate source that provides only calories and *no* other nutrients. Sugar also encourages dental decay.

● Increase fibre intake – by eating wholemeal bread, wholegrain products, brown rice, bran products, beans, pulses, fruit and vegetables. Fibre has been shown to help in the prevention of bowel disorders, such as constipation and diverticulitis.

● Increase intake of fruit and vegetables – to provide fibre and carbohydrate in a form which also supplies vitamins and minerals (unlike sugar).

● Decrease salt intake – avoid eating too many highly salted processed foods. Reduce amount of salt added during cooking or at the table. High sodium levels can increase blood pressure, which is implicated in cerebro-vascular disease (stroke).

● Moderate alcohol intake. Alcohol provides a high number of calories with few other nutrients.

● Try the healthy menus and recipes on the following pages. They will be a good start in reshaping your eating habits.

FAMILY WINTER WEEKEND MENUS

SATURDAY

Breakfast: Dried Fruit Compote*
Sunflower Seed Bread* with Honey
Herb Tea

Lunch: Pizza
Cauliflower and Watercress Salad*
Bananas with Yogurt and Honey

Children's Tea: Jacket Potatoes Stuffed with Bacon and
   Cheese
Carrot Salad
Prune and Apple Cake*

Parents' Dinner: Crudités with Avocado Mayonnaise
   (sticks of raw vegetables served with
   mayonnaise flavoured with 1 mashed
   avocado, as a dip)
Chicken with Mushrooms*
Brown Rice
Green Salad
Apricot Wholemeal Crêpes*

SUNDAY

Breakfast: Apple Juice
Granola* with Yogurt
Wholemeal Bread with Honey
Herb Tea

Lunch: Roast Chicken with Herbs and Garlic
Potatoes Lyonnaise
   (sliced potatoes and onions layered
   in a dish and baked)
Brussels Sprouts
Wholemeal Blackberry Crumble*

High Tea: Toasted Sandwiches
Wholemeal Cheese Scones*
Wholemeal Sponge Cake*
Muesli Bars*

Recipes given on pages 73-79 and 90-93

FAMILY SUMMER WEEKEND MENUS

SATURDAY

Breakfast: Watermelon Compote
(cubes of melon flavoured with
honey and lemon juice)
Wholemeal Bread and Honey
Herb Tea

Picnic Lunch: Wholemeal Spinach Pie*
Tomato and Chive Salad
(thinly sliced tomatoes tossed in
Chive Dressing – see page 91)
Yogurt and Fresh Fruit

Children's Tea: Hamburgers in Wholemeal Buns
Green Salad
Apricot Slices*

Parents' Dinner: Tomato and Basil Soup*
Lamb Kebabs
(cubes of grilled lamb, onion, green
pepper and tomato)
Brown Rice
Green Salad
Strawberry and Yogurt Crunch*

SUNDAY

Breakfast: Banana Granola*
Wholemeal Bread and Honey
Herb Tea

Barbecue Lunch: Barbecued Chicken
Broccoli and Bean Sprout Salad*
Baked Potatoes with Soured Cream
Baked Bananas with Rum

Tea: Double Decker Sandwich
Wholemeal Cheese Scones*
Wholemeal Sponge Cake*

Recipes given on pages 73-79 and 90-93

EVENING MEALS FOR SUMMER WEEKDAYS

Courgettes au Gratin*
Spinach and Mushroom Salad
Wholemeal Strawberry Sponge*

Grilled Trout with Herbs
Baby New Potatoes with Peas
Watermelon Sorbet*

Mushroom and Watercress Soup*
Salade Niçoise with crusty Wholemeal Bread
Fresh Fruit

Grilled Chicken with Herbs
New Potatoes
Spinach
Strawberries with Yogurt Snow*

Stuffed Aubergines*
Green Salad
Summer Fruit Salad*

EVENING MEALS FOR WINTER WEEKDAYS

Leek and Lentil Patties with Tomato Sauce*
Brown Rice
Baked Apples stuffed with Dates

Chicken and Red Pepper Pie*
Red Cabbage and Radish Salad*
Date and Apple Whip*

Vegetable Casserole*
Jacket Potatoes
Prune and Apple Cake*

Pear and Grape Vinaigrette*
Monkfish Américaine*
Brown Rice and Green Salad
Selection of Cheeses

Pork and Bean Ragoût*
Chinese Cabbage Salad
Fruit and Nut Salad*

Recipes given on pages 73-79 and 90-93

GRANOLA

120 ml (4 fl oz) safflower oil
90 ml (3 fl oz) malt extract
90 ml (3 fl oz) clear honey
250 g (8 oz) rolled oats
250 g (8 oz) jumbo oats
125 g (4 oz) hazelnuts
25 g (1 oz) desiccated coconut
50 g (2 oz) sunflower seeds
25 g (1 oz) sesame seeds

Place the oil, malt and honey in a large pan and heat gently until the malt is runny. Mix in the remaining ingredients and stir thoroughly.

Turn into a large roasting pan and bake in a preheated moderately hot oven, 190°C (375°F), Gas Mark 5, for 30 to 35 minutes, stirring occasionally so that it browns evenly. Allow to cool.

Store in an airtight container. Serve with natural yogurt.
MAKES ABOUT 1 KG (2 LB)

Banana Granola: Mix 125 g (4 oz) granola with 300 g (10.4 oz) natural yogurt and 1 sliced banana. SERVES 4.

DRIED FRUIT COMPOTE

250 g (8 oz) mixed dried fruits
50 g (2 oz) dried apricots
450 ml (¾ pint) apple juice

Place the dried fruits in a bowl with the apple juice and leave to soak overnight. Cover and simmer gently for 15 minutes, then pour into a serving bowl and cool.

Serve chilled, with yogurt.
SERVES 4

Fruit and Nut Salad: Simmer the fruit as above, adding 1 teaspoon ground cinnamon. Leave to cool, then add 2 sliced bananas and sprinkle with 25 g (1 oz) toasted flaked almonds.

MUSHROOM AND WATERCRESS SOUP

2 tablespoons olive oil
1 large onion, chopped
125 g (4 oz) button mushrooms, sliced
1 tablespoon flour
1 × 425 g (15 oz) can consommé
450 ml (¾ pint) water
1 bunch of watercress, chopped
salt and pepper

Heat the oil in a pan, add the onion and fry until softened. Add the mushrooms and fry for 2 minutes, then stir in the flour. Add the consommé, water, watercress,
and salt and pepper to taste; simmer for 10 minutes. Serve hot.
SERVES 4 TO 6.

COURGETTES AU GRATIN

3 tablespoons olive oil
2 onions, chopped
750 g (1½ lb) courgettes, sliced
2 cloves garlic, crushed
6 tomatoes, skinned and chopped
1 tablespoon tomato purée
2 tablespoons chopped parsley
salt and pepper
50 g (2 oz) wholemeal breadcrumbs
125 g (4 oz) Cheddar cheese, grated

Heat the oil in a pan, add the onions and courgettes and fry for 10 minutes, stirring occasionally. Add the garlic, tomatoes, tomato purée, parsley, and salt and pepper to taste. Cover and simmer for 15 to 20 minutes, then turn into a 1.5 litre (2½ pint) ovenproof dish.

Mix the breadcrumbs with the cheese and sprinkle over the courgettes to cover completely. Brown under a preheated hot grill for about 5 minutes.
SERVES 4

LEEK AND LENTIL PATTIES

3 tablespoons olive oil
2 leeks, thinly sliced
2 celery sticks, chopped
250 g (8 oz) brown lentils
600 ml (1 pint) water
1 tablespoon soy sauce
salt and pepper
2 tablespoons chopped parsley
125 g (4 oz) wholemeal
   breadcrumbs
oil for shallow-frying
TOMATO SAUCE:
1 × 397 g (14 oz) can tomatoes
2 cloves garlic
1 tablespoon chopped parsley
1 bay leaf

Heat the oil in a pan, add the leeks and celery and fry slowly until softened, stirring occasionally. Add the lentils, water, soy sauce, and salt and pepper to taste and bring to the boil. Cover and simmer for 50 minutes to 1 hour, stirring occasionally. Mix in the parsley and half the breadcrumbs; turn onto a plate to cool.

With wet hands, shape the mixture into 12 patties and coat with remaining breadcrumbs.

Pour oil into a frying pan to a depth of 5 mm (¼ inch) and place over a moderate heat. When hot, add the patties and fry until crisp and golden brown, turning once.

To make the sauce, place the tomatoes with their juice in a pan, stirring well to break up the tomatoes. Add the remaining ingredients, with salt and pepper to taste, and simmer for 15 minutes. Serve with the patties.

SERVES 4

CHICKEN AND RED PEPPER PIE

2 tablespoons oil
1 onion, chopped
1 clove garlic, crushed
50 g (2 oz) mushrooms, sliced
3 celery sticks, sliced
1 red pepper, cored, seeded and
   sliced
1 tablespoon flour
300 ml (½ pint) chicken stock
500 g (1 lb) cooked chicken,
   shredded
salt and pepper
250 g (8 oz) wholemeal pastry (see
   opposite page)
beaten egg to glaze

Heat the oil in a pan, add the onion and fry until softened. Add the garlic, mushrooms, celery and red pepper and cook for 5 to 8 minutes, stirring occasionally. Remove from the heat and stir in the flour. Pour in the stock and stir until blended. Return to the heat and bring to the boil, stirring, until thickened. Stir in the chicken, and salt and pepper to taste. Transfer to a 1.2 litre (2 pint) pie dish and leave to cool.

Roll out the pastry to a shape about 5 cm (2 inches) larger than the dish. Cut off a narrow strip all round and place on the dampened edge of the dish. Dampen the strip then cover with the pastry, sealing well. Trim and flute the edges, decorate with pastry leaves made from the trimmings and make a hole in the centre. Brush with egg and bake in a preheated moderately hot oven, 200°C (400°F), Gas Mark 6, for 30 minutes. Serve hot.

SERVES 4

PORK AND BEAN RAGOÛT

4 tablespoons oil
350 g (12 oz) lean pork, cut into
2.5 cm (1 inch) cubes
2 onions, sliced
350 g (12 oz) black beans, soaked
overnight and drained
750 ml (1¼ pints) water
2 celery sticks
2 cloves garlic, crushed
1 × 397 g (14 oz) can tomatoes
1 bay leaf
1 red pepper, cored, seeded and
chopped
2 tablespoons chopped parsley
salt and pepper

Heat half the oil in a flameproof casserole, add the meat and fry briskly until sealed. Remove from the pan and set aside. Heat the remaining oil, then add the onions and fry until softened. Add the beans and water, cover, bring to the boil and simmer for 30 minutes.

Return the meat to the pan with the celery, garlic, tomatoes with their juice and bay leaf. Cover and cook in a preheated moderate oven, 180°C (350°F), Gas Mark 4, for 45 minutes.

Stir in the red pepper, parsley, and salt and pepper to taste, then return to the oven for 30 minutes, until the beans are soft.

SERVES 4

WHOLEMEAL SPINACH PIE

PASTRY:
350 g (12 oz) wholemeal flour
1 teaspoon salt
175 g (6 oz) margarine or butter
3-4 tablespoons iced water
beaten egg to glaze
FILLING:
2 tablespoons olive oil
1 large onion, chopped
2 cloves garlic, crushed
4 × 227 g (8 oz) packets frozen
chopped spinach, slightly thawed
1 egg, beaten
½ teaspoon grated nutmeg
50 g (2 oz) grated Parmesan cheese
salt and pepper

First prepare the filling. Heat the oil in a pan, add the onion and fry until softened. Add the garlic and spinach, cover and cook gently for 10 minutes, stirring occasionally. Remove the lid and cook for a further 5 minutes. Cool slightly, then beat in the egg, nutmeg, cheese, and salt and pepper to taste. Cool completely.

Meanwhile, make the pastry as for Apricot slices (see page 77). Cut off two thirds of the dough, roll out thinly on a floured surface and use to line a 23 cm (9 inch) shallow pie plate.

Turn the filling into the prepared dish and spread evenly. Dampen the pastry edges. Roll out the remaining pastry thinly and place in position for the lid, sealing well. Trim and flute the edges, decorate with pastry leaves made from the trimmings and make a hole in the centre. Chill for 15 minutes. Brush with beaten egg and bake in a preheated moderately hot oven, 200°C (400°F), Gas Mark 6, for 45 to 50 minutes.

Serve hot or cold with a salad.

SERVES 6

STUFFED AUBERGINES

2 large aubergines
2 tablespoons olive oil
1 large onion, chopped
2 cloves garlic, crushed
250 g (8 oz) mushrooms, sliced
50 g (2 oz) brown rice, cooked
2 tablespoons tomato purée
50 g (2 oz) cashew nuts, chopped
2 tablespoons chopped parsley
salt and pepper
75 g (3 oz) Cheddar cheese, grated

Prick the aubergines all over with a fork, cut in half and place cut side down on a greased baking sheet. Bake in a preheated moderately hot oven, 190°C (375°F), Gas Mark 5, for 30 minutes.

Meanwhile, heat the oil in a pan, add the onion and fry until softened. Add the garlic and mushrooms and fry over a gentle heat for 3 minutes. Add the rice, tomato purée, nuts, parsley, and salt and pepper to taste. Mix well and heat through gently while preparing the aubergines.

Scoop the flesh from the aubergines, without breaking the skin, chop finely and mix with the rice mixture. Pile into the aubergine skins, sprinkle with the cheese and bake for 10 minutes, until the cheese has melted.
SERVES 4

APRICOT WHOLEMEAL CRÊPES

BATTER:
125 g (4 oz) wholemeal flour
1 egg
300 ml (½ pint) milk
1 tablespoon oil
FILLING:
250 g (8 oz) dried apricots, chopped
  and soaked for 2 hours
2 teaspoons arrowroot
1 tablespoon clear honey
TO FINISH:
2 tablespoons clear honey
25 g (1 oz) flaked almonds, toasted
TO SERVE:
Yogurt snow (see page 93)

Place the flour, egg and milk in an electric blender or food processor and work for 30 seconds, until the batter is smooth.

Heat a 15 cm (6 inch) omelet pan and add 1 teaspoon of the oil. When hot, pour in 1 tablespoon of the batter and tilt the pan to coat the bottom evenly. Cook until the underside is brown, then turn and cook for 10 seconds. Repeat with the remaining batter, stacking the pancakes as they cook.

To make the filling, place the apricots and their soaking liquid in a pan, cover and simmer for 10 minutes. Mix the arrowroot with a little water, stir into the apricots with the honey and cook, stirring, until thickened.

Place a little filling on each pancake, roll up and arrange in an ovenproof dish.

Warm the honey and spoon over the pancakes to glaze. Place in a preheated moderate oven, 180°C (350°F), Gas Mark 4, for 10 to 15 minutes, until heated through. Sprinkle with the almonds and serve with the Yogurt snow.
SERVES 4

WHOLEMEAL BLACKBERRY CRUMBLE

175 g (6 oz) wholemeal flour
75 g (3 oz) margarine
125 g (4 oz) raw sugar
50 g (2 oz) hazelnuts, chopped
350 g (12 oz) dessert apples, peeled and cored
350 g (12 oz) blackberries

Place the flour in a mixing bowl and rub in the margarine until the mixture resembles breadcrumbs. Stir in 75 g (3 oz) of the sugar and the hazelnuts.

Slice the apples and mix with the blackberries and remaining sugar. Turn into a 900 ml (1½ pint) pie dish and sprinkle the crumble mixture over the fruit to cover it completely.

Bake in a preheated moderate oven, 180°C (350°F), Gas Mark 4, for 40 to 50 minutes, until golden brown.

Serve hot or cold, with natural yogurt sweetened with honey.
SERVES 4 TO 6

APRICOT SLICES

250 g (8 oz) wholemeal flour
125 g (4 oz) margarine or butter
2-3 tablespoons water
FILLING:
125 g (4 oz) margarine or butter
75 g (3 oz) raw sugar
2 eggs
50 g (2 oz) wholemeal flour
175 g (6 oz) dried apricots, chopped and soaked for 2 hours
125 g (4 oz) ground almonds
½ teaspoon almond essence
50 g (2 oz) flaked almonds

Place the flour in a mixing bowl and rub in the fat until the mixture resembles breadcrumbs. Stir in enough water to mix to a firm dough. Turn onto a floured surface and knead lightly. Roll out thinly and use to line a 30 × 20 cm (12 × 8 inch) Swiss roll tin. Chill for 15 minutes.

Meanwhile, cream the fat and sugar together until fluffy, then beat in the eggs one at a time, adding half the flour with each one. Drain the apricots and dry on kitchen paper. Stir into the mixture with the ground almonds and essence. Place in the prepared tin and smooth evenly to the edges. Sprinkle the almonds on top.

Bake in a preheated moderately hot oven, 190°C (375°F), Gas Mark 5, for 40 to 45 minutes, until golden. Cool in the tin for a few minutes, then place carefully on a wire rack to cool completely. Cut into slices to serve.
MAKES 18

MUESLI BARS

125 g (4 oz) butter or margarine
90 ml (3 fl oz) clear honey
350 g (12 oz) muesli
2 tablespoons sesame seeds

Place the fat and honey in a large pan and heat gently until melted. Stir in the muesli and sesame seeds and mix thoroughly.

Turn into a greased 18 × 28 cm (7 × 11 inch) baking tin and smooth the top with a wet palette knife.

Bake in a preheated moderate oven, 180°C (350°F), Gas Mark 4, for 20 to 25 minutes.

Cool in the tin for 2 minutes, then cut into bars. Cool for a further 15 minutes, then remove from the tin.
MAKES 16

NOTE: The sweetness of these bars will depend on the type of muesli used. If liked, add 1 to 2 tablespoons raw sugar.

PRUNE AND APPLE CAKE

125 g (4 oz) stoned prunes, chopped
150 ml (¼ pint) water
125 g (4 oz) soft brown sugar
120 ml (4 fl oz) corn oil
2 eggs
150 g (5 oz) wholemeal flour
½ teaspoon bicarbonate of soda
1 teaspoon ground mixed spice
1 teaspoon ground cinnamon
120 ml (4 fl oz) natural yogurt
1 dessert apple, cored and grated
25 g (1 oz) walnuts, chopped

Grease a 20 cm (8 inch) deep cake tin, line the base with grease-proof paper and grease again.

Place the prunes in a pan with the water, cover and simmer gently for 10 minutes. Stir in the sugar and allow to cool.

Stir in the remaining ingredients, except the walnuts, and beat together thoroughly. Pour the mixture into the prepared tin and sprinkle the walnuts on top.

Bake in a preheated moderate oven, 180°C (350°F), Gas Mark 4, for 30 minutes, until firm to the touch.

Remove from the tin and peel off the lining paper. Serve hot as a dessert, or cold as a cake.

SERVES 6 TO 8

WHOLEMEAL CHEESE SCONES

125 g (4 oz) wholemeal flour
125 g (4 oz) plain flour
1 teaspoon cream of tartar
½ teaspoon bicarbonate of soda
½ teaspoon salt
pinch of cayenne pepper
1 teaspoon dry mustard
50 g (2 oz) butter or margarine
125 g (4 oz) Cheddar cheese, grated
120 ml (4 fl oz) milk
  (approximately)

Place the wholemeal flour in a mixing bowl, then sift in the plain flour and remaining dry ingredients. Rub in the fat until the mixture resembles bread-crumbs, then stir in 75 g (3 oz) of the cheese and enough milk to mix to a soft dough.

Turn onto a floured surface, knead lightly and roll out to a 2 cm (¾ inch) thickness. Cut into 5 cm (2 inch) rounds with a plain cutter and place on a floured baking sheet. Sprinkle with the remaining cheese.

Bake in a preheated moderately hot oven, 200°C (400°F), Gas Mark 6, for 15 minutes. Transfer to a wire rack to cool. Serve split and buttered.

MAKES 10

WHOLEMEAL SPONGE CAKE

2 eggs
75 g (3 oz) soft brown sugar
1 teaspoon ground cinnamon
50 g (2 oz) wholemeal flour
1 tablespoon corn oil
FILLING:
1 tablespoon clear honey
2 tablespoons apple juice
1/2 teaspoon ground cinnamon
3 dessert apples, cored and sliced

Line the base of a 20 cm (8 inch) sandwich tin, then grease and flour.

Whisk the eggs and sugar together in an electric blender or food processor until thick and mousse-like. Sift the cinnamon into the flour, then carefully fold into the whisked mixture with a metal spoon. Fold in the oil, then turn into the prepared tin.

Bake in a preheated moderately hot oven, 190°C (375°F), Gas Mark 5, for 20 to 25 minutes, until the cake springs back when lightly pressed. Turn onto a wire rack to cool.

To make the filling, place the honey and apple juice in a heavy-based pan. Add the cinnamon and apples, cover and simmer gently for 5 minutes, stirring occasionally. Leave in the pan until cold.

Split the cake in half horizontally and sandwich together with the filling.

MAKES ONE 20 CM (8 INCH) CAKE

VARIATIONS:
Whisk 4 tablespoons double cream and spread over the cake and top with the filling.
Wholemeal Strawberry Sponge: Whisk 142 ml (5 fl oz) double cream, fold in 125 g (4 oz) sliced strawberries and 1 teaspoon clear honey and use to sandwich the cakes together.

SUNFLOWER SEED BREAD

750 g (1 1/2 lb) wholemeal flour
750 g (1 1/2 lb) granary flour
3 teaspoons salt
75 g (3 oz) sunflower seeds
25 g (1 oz) fresh yeast
900 ml-1.2 litres (1 1/2-2 pints)
* warm water*
2 tablespoons malt extract
2 tablespoons sunflower oil

Mix the flours, salt and all but 2 tablespoons of the sunflower seeds together in a mixing bowl. Chop the reserved sunflower seeds and set aside. Cream the yeast with a little of the water and leave until frothy. Add to the flour mixture with the remaining water, malt extract and oil; mix to a soft dough.

Turn onto a floured surface and knead for 5 minutes until smooth and elastic. Place in a bowl, cover with a damp cloth and leave to rise in a warm place for about 1 1/2 hours until doubled in size.

Turn onto a floured surface and knead for a few minutes, then divide into 4 pieces. Shape and place each piece in a greased 500 g/1 lb loaf tin. Brush with water and sprinkle with the chopped sunflower seeds.

Cover loosely and leave to rise in a warm place for about 30 minutes until the dough just reaches the top of the tins. Bake in a preheated hot oven, 220°C (425°F), Gas Mark 7, for 15 minutes. Lower the temperature to 190°C (375°F), Gas Mark 5, and bake for a further 20 minutes or until the bread sounds hollow when tapped. Turn onto a wire rack to cool.

MAKES FOUR 500 G (1 LB) LOAVES

Slimming

At the present time approximately 40% of the adult population is overweight and there is an increasing number of children who are overweight. We become overweight when our intake of calories is greater than those used, so the excess is converted to fat and stored in the body. The solution to this problem is to reduce the number of calories taken in and increase activity to use more calories. Increasing activity alone is not very successful because each pound of fat represents 3,500 calories which would mean hours of exercise!

'Crash' diets – where only very few calories are taken in usually as one or two foods – are not very wise because they can only be maintained for a short time. They can be dangerous, in that they affect the metabolic balance of the body, and are usually not very successful because the main weight loss is due to body fluid not fat. If this type of diet is prolonged, the body's protein-rich stores start to break down, i.e. muscles. It is much wiser to aim at losing about 1 kg (2 lb) a week which requires a reduction of about 1,000 calories a day.

The body requires at least 800-1,000 calories per day for ordinary functioning so for weight reduction there should be a calorie intake of: 1,000-1,200 for women and 1,200-1,500 for men. Anyone reducing the amount of food they are eating must keep a close check that their requirements for proteins, vitamins, minerals and fibre are met. Anyone who has a known medical condition or is taking some form of medication should always seek the advice of a doctor or dietician before commencing any diet.

Some Useful Hints to Help Dieting
- Weigh yourself once a week only, on the same day, at the same time, preferably without clothes and using the same scales. The scales must be accurate. To check, place a fixed, known weight on the centre, take the reading and adjust if necessary. Move your scales as little as possible.
- Try to have three meals a day with a protein food at each meal.
- Always sit down at a table and eat food with a knife and fork.
- Don't eat snacks between meals. If really necessary have an extra drink – water, tea, coffee, bovril, oxo, lemon juice – or eat a piece of fruit, a tomato, or a stick of celery.
- Take in plenty of fluids.

Calorie controlled diets

You can count all your calorie intake by weighing all of the food you eat. Alternatively you should be able to cut calories by following this plan:

Eat average helpings of:

Lean meat – about 125 g (4 oz)	Beef, veal, pork, lamb, rabbit, liver, kidney, bacon, ham, chicken, etc (lean only).
Fish – about 150 g (5 oz)	All types including shellfish.
Eggs	Boiled or poached (1 egg); scrambled or as a small omelet (2 eggs).
Cheese – 25-50 g (1-2 oz)	All except cream cheese.

Eat or drink as much as you like of:

Vegetables	Cabbage, cauliflower, French or runner beans, broccoli, kale, spinach, Brussels sprouts, etc.
Salads	Lettuce, tomato, celery, radish, cucumber, etc.
Fresh fruit	Apples, oranges, pears, grapes.
Seasonings	Vinegar, herbs, spices.
Drinks	Water, soda water, sugar-free drinks, pure lemon juice, tea and coffee without sugar and using milk from the daily allowance.
Sweetener	Liquid or tablet low-calorie sweeteners.

Do NOT eat:

Sugary foods	Sugar, sweets, chocolates, ice-cream, cakes, biscuits, jams, jellies, marmalade, honey, lemon curd, tinned fruit in syrup, milk drinks, drinking chocolate and flavoured yogurt.
Starchy foods	Cakes, biscuits, pasta foods, semolina, rice, pies, thickened sauces, custard.
Fatty foods	All fried foods, meat fat, sausages, nuts, crisps, cooking oils and fats, salad dressing, mayonnaise, cream, evaporated and condensed milk, cream cheese.
Drinks	All containing sugar, glucose or alcohol, e.g. lager, beer, wine, liqueurs, fizzy drinks, Lucozade, squash, sweetened fruit juice, Ribena, malted and bedtime drinks.

Adhere to daily and weekly allowances of butter, margarine, milk and bread.

An outline of a calorie controlled diet

Butter or margarine – 125 g (4 oz) per week – to supply vitamin A and D requirements.

Milk – 200-300 ml (⅓-½ pint) milk or 400-600 ml (⅔-1 pint) skimmed milk per day.

Bread – 3 large thin slices of wholemeal bread per day.

Breakfast
½ grapefruit
1 egg, poached or boiled
2 tomatoes
1 slice wholemeal bread
(from daily allowance)

Mid-day meal
Average helping of lean meat
or fish or egg or cheese
Plenty of steamed or boiled
vegetables or salad
2 slices wholemeal bread
(from daily allowance)
1 apple

Evening meal
Average helping of lean meat
or fish or egg or cheese
Plenty of steamed or boiled
vegetables or salad
1-2 boiled or jacket potatoes
(the size of an egg)
1 orange

Children require more calories and vitamins because of growth so allow 600 ml (1 pint) milk and more fruit and vegetables. Men require more calories so allow an extra 1 or 2 slices of bread and 1 or 2 potatoes and more fruit and vegetables.

SUMMER CALORIE CONTROLLED DIET PLAN

	Monday	Tuesday	Wednesday	Thursday	Friday	Saturday	Sunday
Breakfast	1 small glass unsweetened fruit juice 2 tbsp muesli with milk	½ grapefruit 1 poached egg 1 slice bread	fresh fruit in 150 g (5 oz) natural low fat yogurt 1 slice bread	1 small glass unsweetened fruit juice 1 boiled egg 1 slice bread	½ grapefruit 25 g (1 oz) cheese on 1 slice toast	1 small glass unsweetened fruit juice 2 tbsp branflakes with milk	½ grapefruit 2 rashers lean bacon, grilled 2 tomatoes 1 slice bread
Light meal	125 g (4 oz) lean meat salad 2 slices bread 1 nectarine	1 × 150 g (5 oz) smoked mackerel fillet salad 2 slices toast cherries	25 g (1 oz) cheese salad 2 slices bread 1 small bunch grapes	125 g (4 oz) cottage cheese tomato cucumber 2 slices bread 3 plums	125 g (4 oz) roast chicken salad 2 slices bread 4-6 strawberries	tomatoes stuffed with 125 g (4 oz) cottage cheese salad 2 slices bread 1 peach	125 g (4 oz) ham salad 2 slices bread 1 slice melon
Main meal	1 slice melon 150 g (5 oz) mixed shellfish salad 1 slice bread strawberries and raspberries with 150 g (5 oz) natural low fat yogurt	Pear & Grape Vinaigrette* 2-egg omelet seasonal vegetables 1-2 new potatoes Lemon sorbet	Grapefruit cocktail 125 g (4 oz) Tandoori chicken piece 2 tbsp brown rice salad 1 peach	Vichyssoise 125 g (4 oz) roast meat 1-2 new potatoes seasonal vegetables Summer Fruit Salad*	Florida cocktail 150 g (5 oz) tuna fish (canned in brine) salad 1 slice bread natural low fat yogurt with 1 tbsp muesli	1 small glass unsweetened fruit juice 125 g (4 oz) cold roast beef Broccoli and Bean sprout Salad* 1 slice bread Watermelon Sorbet*	Tomato and Basil Soup* 125 g (4 oz) grilled liver rice green salad Strawberry and Yogurt Crunch*

NOTE: All bread and milk must be taken from the daily allowance; all butter or margarine must be taken from the weekly allowance. These are given on page 83. Recipes marked with an asterisk are given on pages 90-93.

WINTER CALORIE CONTROLLED DIET PLAN

	Monday	Tuesday	Wednesday	Thursday	Friday	Saturday	Sunday
Breakfast	1 small glass unsweetened fruit juice 3 tbsp branflakes with milk	½ grapefruit 1 boiled egg 1 slice wholemeal bread	2 tbsp muesli with milk 1 slice toast 2 tomatoes	½ grapefruit 2 rashers lean bacon, grilled 2 tomatoes 1 slice toast	1 small glass unsweetened fruit juice 1 poached egg 2 tbsp baked beans	3 tbsp porridge with milk fresh fruit	1 small glass unsweetened fruit juice 150 g (5 oz) kipper with grilled mushrooms 1 slice bread
Light meal	2 slices cheese on toast, using 25 g (1 oz) cheese 1 apple	cauliflower with 50 g (2 oz) melted cheese 1 slice bread 1 orange	1 poached egg on vegetables 1 slice bread 1 apple	150 g (5 oz) canned salmon salad 1 banana	150 g (5 oz) any smoked fish 2 tbsps brown rice, cooked 1 pear	2 tbsps baked beans on 1 slice toast 1 orange	2-egg omelet 2 tomatoes 1 slice bread 1 pear
Main meal	Mushroom and Watercress soup* Monkfish Americaine* 1 boiled potato vegetables Dried fruit compote	Tomato and Basil Soup* 150 g (5 oz) any poached white fish 2 tbsps brown rice, cooked Date and Apple Whip*	150 g (5 oz) natural low fat yogurt with cucumber 125 g (4 oz) grilled liver 2 tbsps brown rice, cooked Poached pears	½ grapefruit Vegetable Casserole* 2 slices bread 150 g (5 oz) natural low fat yogurt with 25 g (1 oz) nuts	Onion soup 175 g (6 oz) pork chop, grilled 1 jacket potato red cabbage Stewed fruit	Pear & Grape Vinaigrette* Chicken with Mushrooms* 1-2 boiled potatoes vegetables fresh fruit	Grapefruit cocktail 125 g (4 oz) roast turkey 1-2 boiled potatoes Cauliflower and Watercress Salad* Baked apple

NOTE: All bread and milk must be taken from the daily allowance; all butter or margarine must be taken from the weekly allowance. These are given on page 83. Recipes marked with an asterisk are given on pages 90-93.

Alternative Diets

People often say they cannot keep to a calorie controlled diet because they can't be bothered to count the calories. Other diets which will help reduce weight are ones that restrict certain foods.

Low Carbohydrate Diet

Instead of considering calories, try to keep carbohydrates to: 60-100 g (2-3.5 oz) per day for women and 105-120 g (3.7-4.2 oz) per day for men and children.

To reduce carbohydrate, exclude sugar and starchy foods, i.e. sugar, biscuits, cakes, bread, cereals, rice, noodles, spaghetti, savoury snacks, sugary beverages, alcoholic drinks, jams, honey, sweets, thick sauces, soups, puddings, ice-cream.

Foods that can be eaten without limit are lean meat, sausages, fish, eggs, cheese, salads, vegetables, fresh fruit, canned fruit in natural juice, nuts as part of a main meal.

High quantities of protein tend to be eaten in this type of diet; as protein is very satisfying, this helps limit food intake.

Even in a low carbohydrate diet you are allowed 300 ml (½ pint) milk, 15 g (½ oz) butter or margarine, up to 75 g (3 oz) bread and one small helping of cereal product, i.e. rice, spaghetti, cereal, each day.

Here are suggestions for different breakfasts, light meals and main meals. Make up your own menu plans from the choices given below; any variations will still keep you within the recommended limits of carbohydrate intake. All bread, milk and butter or margarine (used for spreading or cooking) must be taken from the daily allowance.

Breakfast

1 small glass tomato juice
or ½ grapefruit
plus 1 egg, poached or boiled
or 1-2 rashers lean grilled bacon
or 125 g (4 oz) kipper fillet
plus 1 crispbread

Light meal

2-egg omelet and salad
or
125 g (4 oz) piece chicken
plus salad
or 125 g (4 oz) tuna
(canned in brine) plus salad
plus 1 piece of citrus fruit
or 1 wedge of melon

Main meal

Tomato and Basil Soup★
or Pear and Grape Vinaigrette★
or ½ grapefruit
plus Vegetable Casserole★ (no potato)
or 175 g (6 oz) pork chop, grilled, plus vegetables and 1-2 small boiled potatoes
or 125 g (4 oz) piece golden haddock, plus 1 poached egg, vegetables and 1 slice wholemeal bread
plus stewed fruit (using low calorie sweetener)
or ½ low fat natural yogurt
or Fresh raspberries and strawberries

Low Fat Diet

In a low fat diet try to reduce the fat intake in the diet. You are still allowed 50 g (2 oz) butter or margarine or 125 g (4 oz) low fat spread per week; this is to ensure adequate intake of vitamins A and D (or a vitamin supplement is necessary). Also allowed is 150 ml (¼ pint) milk or 300 ml (½ pint) skimmed milk, and a maximum of 1 egg per day.

Foods not allowed include: all fried foods, oils and fats, cakes, biscuits, cream, hard cheese, fried snacks such as crisps, high fat content meat products such as pork pie, sausages, salami, etc.

Foods allowed include: lean meat (all visible fat trimmed off), poultry with the skin removed, fish, canned fish in brine (not oil), cottage cheese, bread, rice, spaghetti, pasta, potatoes, and any quantity of fruit and vegetables.

Make up your own menu plans from the choices given below. Bread, milk and butter or margarine (used for spreading or cooking) must be taken from the daily/weekly allowance.

Breakfast
½ grapefruit
or 1 small glass of unsweetened fruit juice
plus 2 tablespoons wheatflakes or branflakes or cornflakes
plus 150 ml (¼ pint) milk
or 1 boiled or poached egg, plus 1 slice wholemeal bread
or 1 rasher of lean bacon, grilled, plus 1 slice wholemeal bread

Light meal
125 g (4 oz) cottage cheese, plus salad and 1 slice wholemeal bread
or 2 tablespoons baked beans on 1 slice wholemeal bread, toasted
or 125 g (4 oz) tuna (canned in brine), plus salad
plus 1 piece of fruit

Main meal
Tomato and Basil Soup★
or 1 wedge of melon
plus Vegetable Casserole★
or 125 g (4 oz) roast chicken (no skin), plus vegetables including 1-2 boiled potatoes
or 150 g (5 oz) poached haddock, plus vegetables including 1-2 boiled potatoes
plus Watermelon Sorbet★
or Fresh fruit
or Stewed fruit

High Fibre Reducing Diet

A high fibre diet makes a useful healthy slimming diet. High fibre foods generally need a lot of chewing so you feel you are eating more but – more important – high fibre foods are bulky so the stomach feels satisfied more quickly.

The basic principles of a calorie controlled diet still hold for a high fibre diet so sweet and sugary foods should be avoided, starchy foods should be restricted, and fatty foods avoided. To increase your fibre intake and reduce calorie intake:

● Substitute wholemeal breakfast cereals for refined cereals. Use Bran Flakes, All Bran, Wheat Flakes, Wholewheat Biscs, porridge.

● Replace white or brown bread with 100% wholemeal bread or Ryvita or brown crispbreads.

● Limit butter and margarine to 125 g (4 oz) maximum per week.

● Have no more than 300 ml (½ pint) milk or 600 ml (1 pint) skimmed milk per day.

● Eat plenty of fruit and vegetables, particularly with the skin and peel on, e.g. jacket potatoes, baked apples. Never peel eating apples or pears.

● Supplement your diet with unprocessed bran by sprinkling a spoonful on cereals, soups, gravy, drinks, vegetables and stewed fruit.

● Use wholemeal spaghetti and pasta.

● Use brown rice.

Make up your own high fibre menu plans from the choices given below, keeping to milk and butter/margarine allowances.

Breakfast
½ grapefruit
or 1 small glass unsweetened fruit juice
plus 2 tablespoons Bran Flakes plus 1 tablespoon bran and 150 ml (¼ pint) milk
or 2 tablespoons muesli plus 1 tablespoon bran and 150 ml (¼ pint) milk
or 1 poached or boiled egg plus 1 slice wholemeal bread

Light meal
2 tablespoons baked beans on 1 slice wholemeal bread, toasted
or 2 slices wholemeal bread, plus 25 g (1 oz) grated cheese and salad
or 50 g (2 oz) wholewheat macaroni cheese, made with cornflour, 150 ml (¼ pint) milk and 25 g (1 oz) cheese
plus 1 banana
or 125 g (4 oz) raspberries

Main meal
Lentil soup
or Pea and ham soup
or 1 tomato stuffed with 50 g (2 oz) cottage cheese
plus Monkfish Américaine★ plus 50 g (2 oz) wholemeal spaghetti
or Vegetable Casserole★ (with kidney beans and 1 tablespoon bran added)
or 125 g (4 oz) grilled gammon steak, plus broad beans or peas and 1 jacket potato
plus 50 g (2 oz) stewed dried fruits (apricots and prunes)
or 150 g (5 oz) natural low fat yogurt with 25 g (1 oz) nuts and 1 tablespoon bran
or Stewed fruit with 1 tablespoon bran

PEAR AND GRAPE VINAIGRETTE

3 tablespoons Chive dressing (see opposite page)
2 ripe dessert pears, peeled and cored
175 g (6 oz) black grapes, halved and seeded
2 oranges, peeled and cut into segments
1 tablespoon sesame seeds, toasted

Place the dressing in a mixing bowl. Slice the pears into the dressing and coat thoroughly. Add the grapes and oranges and toss together. Spoon into individual serving bowls and sprinkle with the sesame seeds to serve.
SERVES 4 TO 6
Calories per portion: 110

TOMATO AND BASIL SOUP

500 g (1 lb) tomatoes, skinned and roughly chopped
1 clove garlic
300 ml (¹/₂ pint) water
300 ml (¹/₂ pint) tomato juice
salt and pepper
1 tablespoon basil, chopped

Place the tomatoes, garlic and water in an electric blender or food processor and work for 30 seconds until smooth. Pour into a tureen, stir in the tomato juice and season liberally with salt and pepper. Mix in half the basil and chill well. Sprinkle with the remaining basil to serve.
SERVES 6
Calories per portion: 21

RED CABBAGE AND RADISH SALAD

2 red dessert apples, quartered and cored
350 g (12 oz) red cabbage, shredded
1 bunch of radishes, thinly sliced
HONEY AND LEMON DRESSING:
2 tablespoons lemon juice
2 tablespoons clear honey
2 tablespoons apple juice
1 tablespoon chopped parsley
salt and pepper

Put all the dressing ingredients, with salt and pepper to taste, in a screw-topped jar and shake well. Pour into a salad bowl.
Slice the apples into the dressing. Add cabbage and radishes, toss well and marinate for 1 to 2 hours, tossing occasionally. Toss again just before serving.
SERVES 6
Calories per portion: 80

CAULIFLOWER AND WATERCRESS SALAD

1 small cauliflower, broken into florets
salt and pepper
1 bunch of watercress
YOGURT DRESSING:
4 tablespoons natural yogurt
1 tablespoon lemon juice
1 clove garlic, crushed
1 teaspoon clear honey
1 tablespoon chopped parsley

Blanch the cauliflower in boiling salted water for 3 minutes. Drain and leave to cool. Place in a salad bowl with the watercress.
Put the dressing ingredients in a screw-topped jar, adding salt and pepper to taste; shake well. Pour over the salad just before serving and toss thoroughly.
SERVES 6
Calories per portion: 40

BROCCOLI AND BEAN SPROUT SALAD

250 g (8 oz) broccoli, broken into
　florets
salt and pepper
175 g (6 oz) bean sprouts
1 small red pepper, cored, seeded
　and sliced
2 tablespoons sesame seeds, toasted
CHIVE DRESSING:
2 tablespoons olive oil
2 teaspoons cider vinegar
1/2 teaspoon clear honey
1/2 teaspoon Dijon mustard
2 tablespoons chopped chives

Blanch the broccoli in boiling
salted water for 4 minutes. Drain
and leave to cool. Place in a salad
bowl with the bean sprouts, red
pepper and sesame seeds.

Put all the dressing ingredients, with salt and pepper to
taste, in a screw-topped jar and
shake well. Pour over the salad
and toss thoroughly to serve.
SERVES 4
Calories per portion: 120

VEGETABLE CASSEROLE

4 tablespoons olive oil
2 onions, sliced
3 celery sticks, sliced
2 teaspoons ground coriander
2 cloves garlic, crushed
3 carrots, sliced
250 g (8 oz) courgettes, sliced
1 small cauliflower, broken into
　florets
1 large potato, cubed
1 × 397 g (14 oz) can tomatoes
1 tablespoon soy sauce
300 ml (1/2 pint) water
salt and pepper
TOPPING:
125 g (4 oz) Cheddar cheese, grated

Heat the oil in a large flameproof
casserole, add the onions and
celery and fry until softened.
Add the coriander and garlic and
fry for 1 minute. Add the remaining vegetables, the tomatoes with
their juice, soy sauce, water, and
salt and pepper to taste. Bring to
the boil and stir well. Cover and
cook in a preheated moderately
hot oven, 190°C (375°F), Gas
Mark 5, for 30 minutes, until
tender.

Sprinkle with the cheese and
place under a preheated hot grill
to brown. Serve immediately.
SERVES 6 TO 8
Calories per portion: 200

MONKFISH AMÉRICAINE

3 tablespoons olive oil
2 onions, chopped
750 g (1½ lb) monkfish, cubed
2 cloves garlic, crushed
2 tablespoons wholemeal flour
500 g (1 lb) tomatoes, skinned and
    chopped
1 tablespoon tomato purée
120 ml (4 fl oz) white wine
120 ml (4 fl oz) water
bouquet garni
salt and pepper
1 tablespoon chopped parsley

Heat the oil in a pan, add the onions and fry until softened. Add the fish and garlic and fry until golden. Remove and set aside.

Add the flour to the pan, stirring well to mix, then add the tomatoes, tomato purée, wine, water, bouquet garni, and salt and pepper to taste. Bring to the boil, stirring, then simmer, uncovered, for 20 minutes. Return the fish to the pan, cover and simmer for 10 to 15 minutes, until tender.

Remove the bouquet garni. Pour into a warmed serving dish and sprinkle with the parsley.

SERVES 4
Calories per portion: 420

CHICKEN WITH MUSHROOMS

350 g (12 oz) chicken breast fillets
4 tablespoons olive oil
2 onions, sliced
250 g (8 oz) button mushrooms,
    sliced
2 tablespoons wholemeal flour
300 ml (½ pint) chicken stock
salt and pepper
2 tablespoons brandy
150 g (5.2 oz) natural yogurt
1 tablespoon chopped parsley

Cut the chicken into 3.5 × 0.5 cm (1½ × ¼ inch) strips. Heat half the oil in a frying pan, add the chicken and fry over high heat, stirring, until sealed. Remove from the pan and set aside.

Heat the remaining oil, add the onions and fry briskly for 2 to 3 minutes, until coloured. Add the mushrooms and cook, stirring, for 1 to 2 minutes. Remove from the heat and stir in the flour. Add the stock and bring to the boil, stirring. Simmer for 2 minutes, then return the chicken to the pan with salt and pepper to taste and cook gently for 5 minutes.

Remove from the heat and pour in the brandy and yogurt. Stir over a low heat until heated through, but do not boil.

Turn into a warmed serving dish and sprinkle with the parsley. Serve with boiled brown rice or a green salad.

SERVES 4
Calories per person: 325

DATE AND APPLE WHIP

*750 g (1½ lb) cooking apples,
  peeled and cored*
3 tablespoons apple juice
1 teaspoon mixed spice
*125 g (4 oz) dates, stoned and
  chopped*
1 egg white
2 tablespoons clear honey
120 ml (4 fl oz) natural yogurt
*2 tablespoons flaked almonds,
  browned*

Slice the apples into a heavy-based pan, add the apple juice and spice, cover and simmer for 10 to 15 minutes. Sieve or work in a blender or food processor until smooth. Turn into a bowl, add the dates and leave to cool.

Whisk the egg white until stiff, then whisk in the honey and continue whisking until very thick. Fold into the apple mixture with the yogurt. Chill until required. Sprinkle with the nuts to serve.
SERVES 6
Calories per portion: 200

STRAWBERRY AND YOGURT CRUNCH

125 g (4 oz) strawberries, sliced
50 g (2 oz) Granola (see page 73)
YOGURT SNOW:
1 egg white
2 tablespoons clear honey
150 g (5.2 oz) natural yogurt

First make the yogurt snow. Whisk the egg white until stiff, then whisk in the honey. Continue whisking until very thick, then carefully fold in the yogurt.

Fold the strawberries into the yogurt snow. Divide half between glasses, sprinkle with Granola, then cover with the remaining yogurt snow. Serve immediately.
SERVES 4
Calories per portion: 140

WATERMELON SORBET

1 × 1.25 kg (2½ lb) watermelon
3 tablespoons clear honey
juice of ½ lemon
1 egg white, stiffly whisked

Scoop out the flesh from the watermelon, discarding the seeds. Place the flesh in an electric blender or food processor with the honey and lemon juice and work until smooth. Pour into a rigid freezerproof container, cover, seal and freeze for 3 to 4 hours, until half frozen.

Turn into a chilled bowl and whisk until fluffy, then gradually whisk in the egg white. Cover, seal and freeze until firm.

Transfer to the refrigerator 15 minutes before serving to soften. Serve in chilled glasses.
SERVES 4
Calories per portion: 100

SUMMER FRUIT SALAD

120 ml (4 fl oz) pineapple juice
1 tablespoon clear honey
125 g (4 oz) strawberries, halved
2 oranges, peeled and segmented
1 banana, sliced
*125 g (4 oz) grapes, halved and
  pipped*
2 kiwi fruit, peeled and thinly sliced
2 tablespoons kirsch
TO SERVE (OPTIONAL):
1 passion fruit
Yogurt snow (see opposite)

Mix the pineapple juice and honey together in a bowl. Add the fruits and kirsch, mix well and chill for 1 to 2 hours.

Halve the passion fruit, scoop out the flesh and fold into the Yogurt snow. Chill for 1 to 2 hours. Serve with the fruit salad.
SERVES 4
Calories per portion: 200
(without yogurt snow: 130)

Index

Abdomen 33; exercises for the 38
Ankles, exercises for the 43, 49
Arm swinging exercise 28

Bath:
   at bedtime 58
   exercising in the 46
Bed, exercising on the 46
Bending exercises 27, 44, 45, 46
Beverages, sleep-inducing 15
Body image 6
Body massage 15
Body types 16
Bottom 33; exercises for the 39
Bran in diet 13
Bust 33; exercises for the 34, 46

Calcium 69
Calorie controlled diets 82-5
Calories 12, 13
Calves, exercises for the 42, 48
Carbohydrates 66, 86-7
Cellulose 66
Chinese pillow 15
Chlorine 69
Constipation 12-13, 58

Dieting, diets 12, 80-93. *See also*
   Recipes
Double chin, exercise for a 46

Eating habits 12-13, 69. *See also*
   Dieting, diets *and* Recipes
Ectomorphs 16, 23
Endomorphs 16, 23
Evening meals (summer) 72
Evening meals (winter) 72
Exercise:
   attitudes to 11
   capacity for 16
   choosing a place for 11
   during and after pregnancy 54-6
   housework and 44-9
   in the office 47-9
   mat, to make 11
Exercises:
   abdomen 38
   ankles 43, 49
   arm swing 28
   bending 27, 44, 45, 46
   bottom 39

   bust 34, 46
   calves 42, 48
   facial 47
   general 26-31
   hips 28, 40
   legs 30, 47, 48
   midriff 36
   posture 8-9
   push-ups 31
   sit-ups 29
   skiing routine 52
   swimming routine 53
   tennis routine 51
   thighs 41, 48
   toe touching 26
   upper arms 35, 47, 49
   waistline 37

Facial exercises 47
facial massage 15
Fats 66
Fibre in diet 69, 88-9
Figure faults, eliminating 33-43
Fitness 10
Folic acid 68

Hair-brushing 15
Head rolling 62
High fibre reducing diet 88-9
Hips 33; exercises for the 28, 40

Indigestion 58
Insomnia, overcoming 58
Iron 69

Jogging 24, 51
Jumping 51

Leg exercises 30, 47, 48
Low carbohydrate diet 86-7
Low fat diet 88-9

Magnesium 69
Massage 15
Measurements 20-3
Menus 70-2. *See also* Recipes
Mesomorphs 16, 23
Metabolism 13
Midriff 33; exercises for the 36
Minerals 68-9
Mobility exercises 24
Muscle strength 24

Neck, exercises for the 15, 49, 62
Nicotinic acid 68

Overweight 69

Phosphorus 69
Posture 8-9
Potassium 69
Pregnancy and afterwards 54-7
Proteins 12, 66
Push-ups 31

Recipes:
  Apricot slices 77
  Apricot wholemeal crêpes 76
  Aubergines, stuffed 76
  Banana granola 73
  Broccoli and bean sprout salad 91
  Cauliflower and watercress salad
    90
  Chicken with mushrooms 92
  Chicken and red pepper pie 74
  Courgettes au gratin 73
  Date and apple whip 93
  Dried fruit compote 73
  Fruit and nut salad 73
  Granola 73
  Leek and lentil patties 74
  Monkfish americaine 92
  Muesli bars 77
  Mushroom and watercress soup 73
  Pear and grape vinaigrette 90
  Pork and bean ragoût 75
  Prune and apple cake 78
  Red cabbage and radish salad 90
  Strawberry sponge cake 79
  Strawberry and yogurt crunch 93
  Summer fruit salad 93
  Sunflower seed bread 79
  Tomato and basil soup 90
  Vegetable casserole 91
  Watermelon sorbet 93
  Wholemeal blackberry crumble 77
  Wholemeal cheese scones 78
  Wholemeal spinach pie 75
  Wholemeal sponge cake 79
Relaxation 58, 60-1. See also Yoga

Riboflavin 68
Running 51

Salt intake, to decrease 69
Scalp massage 15
Shoulders, exercises for the 15, 49
Sit-ups 29
Skiing routine exercise 52
Skipping 51
Sleep 58
Sleep-inducing beverages 15
Slimming and diets 80-93
Sodium 69
Stamina 24
Standing tall 8
Starches 66
Stress 14-15
Stretching exercises 44, 45
Sugars 66
Summer evening meals 72
Summer weekend menus 71
Swimming routine exercise 53

Tennis routine exercise 51
Tension see Stress
Thiamin 15, 68
Thighs 33; exercises for the 41, 48
Toe touch exercise 26

Upper arms 33; exercises for the 35,
  47, 49

Vitamins 13, 68

Waistline 33; exercises for the 37
Walking well 8
Weight 13; correct 18-19
Winter evening meals 72
Winter weekend menus 70

Yoga 62-5
Yogurt 13

Acknowledgments

Photography by Sandra Lousada
Illustrations by Rosalyn Kennedy and Lucy Su
Make up and hair by Carol Hemming
Styling by Alex Anderson
Photographic assistants: Andy Lane and Daphne Wright

The publishers would also like to thank Way In, Harrods and C & A for loan
of clothes, Stirling Cooper Dance Wear Shops for leotards, Fenwicks for
accessories and Bradleys for lingerie, which were used for photography.